Deaf American Poetry

D1559607

Deaf American Poetry

An Anthology

John Lee Clark, *Editor*

Gallaudet University Press   *Washington, DC*

Gallaudet University Press
Washington, DC 20002
http://gupress.gallaudet.edu

The following poets granted permission for the inclusion of their poems in this anthology: Alison Aubrecht, Peter Cook, Willy Conley, Mervin D. Garretson, Abiola Haroun, Christopher Jon Heuer, Kenny Lerner, Raymond Luczak, Katrina R. Miller, Kristi Merriweather, Robert F. Panara, Damara Goff Paris, Debbie Rennie, Kristen Ringman, Curtis Robbins, and Pamela Wright-Meinhardt. I am deeply grateful to them all.

The following individuals and organizations granted permission for the use of poems by deceased poets:

Loy E. Golladay, by permission of June Golladay Amini.

Felix Kowalewski, by permission of the California School for the Deaf at Riverside.

Rex Lowman, by permission of Christine Lowman.

Alice Jane McVan, by permission of the Hispanic Society of America.

Dorothy Miles, by permission of Don Reed.

Linwood Smith, by permission of the National Association of the Deaf.

Library of Congress Cataloging-in-Publication Data

Deaf American poetry : an anthology / John Lee Clark, Editor.
    p. cm.
  Includes bibliographical references.
  ISBN-13: 978-1-56368-413-5
  ISBN-10: 1-56368-413-6
  1. American poetry. 2. Deaf, Writings of the, American. I. Clark, John Lee, 1978–
  PS591.D4D43 2009
  811'.008035272—dc22   2008051965

Cover photograph by Willy Conley, using a technique he calls *watergraph*. Conley takes photographs of water reflections that have been turned upside-down. Depending on environmental factors like the wind, debris in the water, and the color of the sky, each inverted reflection creates a painting framed by whatever was surrounding the water.

Contents

Editor's Note   xiii

Introduction   1

John R. Burnet (1808–1874)   9
    Emma   11

James Nack (1809–1879)   24
    From The Minstrel Boy   26
    The Music of Beauty   37

John Carlin (1813–1891)   38
    The Mute's Lament   40

Mary Toles Peet (1836–1901)   42
    Thoughts on Music   44
    To a Bride   46

Laura C. Redden (1840–1923)   49
    My Story   51
    Thomas Hopkins Gallaudet   53

Angeline Fuller Fischer (1841–1925)   55
    Scenes in the History of the Deaf and Dumb 57
    To a Deaf-Mute Lady   70

Alice Cornelia Jennings (b. 1851)   71

    A Prayer in Signs   73

George M. Teegarden (1852–1936)   75

    The "Nad"   77

    Gallaudet College   78

J. Schuyler Long (1869–1933)   79

    I Wish That I Could Tell   81

Agatha Tiegel Hanson (1873–1959)   83

    Semi-Mute   85

James William Sowell (1875–1949)   86

    The Oralist   88

    Dear Eyes of Grey   89

Howard L. Terry (1877–1964)   90

    From *The Old Homestead*   92

    On My Deafness   97

Alice Jane McVan (1906–1970)   98

    And No Applause   100

    Response   102

Earl Sollenberger (c. 1912–1947)   103

    The Legend of Simon Simplefuss   105

    Birds Will Sing   107

    Reply to "Beware Lest People Think—"   108

Thoughts in a Pennsylvania Cornfield   109

To a Neglected Poet   114

Felix Kowalewski (1913–1989)   115

I Will Take My Dreams . . .   117

Heart of Silence   119

Quasimodo May Not Dare   121

Loy E. Golladay (1914–1999)   122

On Seeing a Poem Recited in Sign Language   124

Silent Homage   125

Footnote to Anthropological Linguistics I   126

Footnote to Anthropological Linguistics II   127

Surely the Phoenix   129

Incident at the B.M.T.   131

Rex Lowman (1918–2001)   133

Bitterweed   135

Beethoven   136

Wingéd Words   137

Robert F. Panara (1920–)   138

On His Deafness   141

Lip Service   142

Idylls of the Green   143

Ars Poetica   151

Mervin D. Garretson (1923–)   152

    for Bill Stokoe   154

    to Doin Hicks   156

    to an expert   157

    deaf again   158

Dorothy Miles (1931–1993)   159

    The Hang-Glider   161

Linwood Smith (1943–1982)   163

    Percy   165

    Mike   166

    The Dream Song of the Deaf Man   167

Curtis Robbins (1943–)   169

    The Rally That Stood the World Still   171

    Solo Dining While Growing Up   173

    The Promised World   174

    Russian Roulette   176

    Deaf Poet or What?   177

Clayton Valli (1951–2003)   178

    A Dandelion   180

    Pawns   181

E. Lynn Jacobowitz (1953–)   183

    In Memoriam: Stephen Michael Ryan   185

Debbie Rennie (1957–)   187

    As Sarah   189

Willy Conley (1958–)   190

    A Deaf Baptism   192

    The Miller of Moments   193

    Salt in the Basement   195

Peter Cook (1962–)   198

    Don Quoxitie Didnt Really

       Attack the Windmill   200

    Ringoes   201

Flying Words Project: Peter Cook and

    Kenny Lerner (est. 1984)   203

    Wise Old Corn #1   205

    Ode to Words   211

Katrina R. Miller (1965–) and

    Damara Goff Paris (1965–)   216

    How the Audist Stole ASL   218

Raymond Luczak (1965–)   223

    The Audiologist   225

    Spelling Bee 1978   226

    Learning to Speak, Part I   229

    Hummingbirds   233

The Crucifixion   234

Instructions to Hearing Persons
     Desiring a Deaf Man   240

Abiola Haroun (1970–)   241

    Deaf Mind   242

    The Deaf Negro   243

    Ode to a Silent World   244

Christopher Jon Heuer (1970–)   245

    Bone Bird   247

    The Hands of My Father   248

    Visible Scars   250

    Diving Bell   252

    Koko Want   253

    We Can Save the Deaf!   255

Kristi Merriweather (1971–)   256

    It Was His Movin' Hands   257

    Be Tellin' Me   259

Pamela Wright-Meinhardt (1971–)   261

    Silent Howl   262

    When They Tell Me . . .   267

John Lee Clark (1978–)   269

    Story Actual Happen   271

    Long Goodbyes   272

The Only Way Signing Can Kill Us   274

My Understanding One Day of Foxgloves   276

Kristen Ringman (1979–)   277

the ear gods   279

Calling Van Gogh   281

Alison L. Aubrecht (1979–)   283

ape-child   284

Conditional Wings   286

What My Teacher Taught Me   288

The Ghost in Yellowed Photographs   291

Hearing-Headed   292

Bibliography   293

Editor's Note

I EMBARKED on this project with the thought of finding poets who reflected in some way, either directly or obliquely, on their deafness or their experiences as deaf people. After canvassing over three hundred volumes of poetry and many periodicals, I found that nonculturally deaf poets, at least in American literature, rarely explore their deafness in their poems. As a result, this book is not an anthology of poetry by just anyone who has a hearing loss; rather, it is drawn from the work of culturally Deaf people who belong to the signing community.*

Collectively, the poems tell the story of the signing community's development and how Deaf people struggled against oppressive forces to discover more about themselves and to celebrate who they are. The growing library of books in Deaf studies is rapidly uncovering much of this epic history, but this book is the only definitive anthology of the work of Deaf poets. Aside from the fact that the poems touch upon a dizzying array of topics, which makes this volume quite a comprehensive introduction for anyone new to Deaf culture and the signing community, the book presents a most important group of Deaf people and preserves what must be considered a significant part of the Deaf literary canon. Deaf poets have contributed to the raising of public awareness about their community and its issues; they have inspired and led other Deaf people, both on and off the page; and their poems have, again and again, crystallized for many of their readers what it means to be Deaf and how to embrace it. No understanding of Deaf culture and its history is complete without an appreciation of Deaf poets and their work.

---

* Since my purpose was not only to gather good poems but also poems relevant to the historical record of deaf people's lives, I will leave the study of nonculturally deaf poets to another scholar.

Questions and challenges peculiar to the relationship between Deaf people and poetry arise from time to time. Foremost among them is the regrettable question, Can Deaf people write poetry? I will respond to this question in the introduction. Some of the other issues include how Deaf poets grapple with expressing themselves through poetry—do they write or sign, and do they conform to or depart from prevailing traditions? How is the ability not only to write correct English but to write poetry used as reassurance to oneself and as a status symbol to others to prove one's intelligence and success in English literacy? Some Deaf people hate poetry because it was shoved down their throats at school, sometimes literally if poetry was used as a speech therapy device, or because they associate it with music, something they automatically assume is out of reach. Many Deaf poets have never been part of a literary community in person, never had the opportunity to network in the publishing world, and often lack access to mentorship, literary events, creative writing programs, and, by extension, grants and fellowships. When the best way to sell poetry books is for the poet to give public readings, many Deaf poets are at a loss as to what to do. Should they read aloud in their nasal, broken speech (if they have any speech) or sign but impose on the bookstore the burden of paying for interpreter costs? And how do they resolve the issue of just how to sign what was written for the page? If they forego public appearances, will they be consigned to oblivion, a literary recluse not by choice but out of necessity?

To complicate matters further, there is the host of issues between Deaf poets and their encounters with discrimination, their varying educational and cultural backgrounds, and their identity politics. Indeed, there is much to say about Deaf poets and their art, too much to fit in this book. I hope my comments, however brief, will encourage readers to do their own in-depth critical analysis of the poems. I also hope this book will serve to increase the recognition and appreciation of Deaf poets both in the reading mainstream and in the signing community.

Acknowledgments

This book, as is true of any other book, would not have been possible without the help of many people. I am deeply grateful to the following for their contributions: Raymond Luczak, for countless hours of typing and research assistance at several libraries; Sara Stallard and Sean Virnig, for gathering and photocopying many books; Ulf Hedberg and Michael Olson of the Gallaudet University Archives, for assistance in locating elusive biographical data; Harry G. Lang, coauthor of *Deaf People in the Arts and Sciences: A Biographical Dictionary*, for additional biographical information; Robert F. Panara, for leads to biographical information on some of his late contemporaries; Joan Naturale of the Wallace Library at Rochester Institute of Technology, for tracking down texts and poets; Judy Yaeger Jones, for sharing with me her important findings about the life of Laura C. Redden; and Jim Cohn of the Museum of American Poetics, for pushing me to dig even deeper. I thank Christian Wiman of *Poetry* magazine for publishing my essay based on the introduction to this book. For their encouragement and support, I am beholden to Alison Aubrecht, Ben Bahan, the late Douglass Bullard, aj granda, Christopher Jon Heuer, Harlan Lane, the late Eric Malzkuhn, Curtis Robbins, Bruce A. White, and Pamela Wright-Meinhardt. Moreover I am indebted to my wife, Adrean, for reasons I do not have the words to capture.

Introduction

THE DEAF POET is no oxymoron, but one might think so, given the popular understanding that poetry has sound and voice at its heart. Add to this the popular philosophy that says deafness reduces human experience. As a result of such ideas, Deaf poets are often objects of amazement or dismissal, their work rarely judged for its merit beyond the context of their deafness. Deaf poets in America always have had to contend with sound, not only as a major factor in why mainstream culture considers Deaf people a lesser variety of the human race, but also as it relates to their chosen art.

This marginalization was especially acute in the nineteenth century, when demands for metrical verse were in force. Such requirements so discouraged Deaf poet John Carlin that he considered giving up on poetry. "I was convinced," he wrote, "that I could never be what I so ardently desired—a correct writer of verses."[1] Fortunately, the perceptive hearing poet William Cullen Bryant pressed Carlin to continue writing poetry, recommending that he rely on rhyming dictionaries. Carlin eventually published many poems, including "The Mute's Lament" in the first issue of *American Annals of the Deaf and Dumb* in 1847. However, the hearing editor could not resist adding a note to the poem, marveling

> How shall he who has not now and who never has had the sense of hearing, who is totally without what the musicians call an ear, succeed in preserving all the niceties of accent, measure, and rhythm? We should almost as soon expect a man born blind to become a landscape painter as one born deaf to produce poetry of even tolerable merit.[2]

In addition to this kind of treatment, Deaf poet Laura C. Redden experienced the opposite. That the acclaimed "Howard Glyndon," Redden's nom de plume, was a woman was well known, but few people knew that she was Deaf. When critics did learn of the fact, however, many of them lowered their earlier opinion of Redden's poetry. Infuriated, Redden responded with her 1870 autobiographical allegory "Down Low" (later retitled "The Realm of Singing"), in which she portrays herself as a bird with a crippled wing trying to make a place for herself in the fabled Realm of Singing. After some attempts, the bird wins an audience of soldiers passing through the forest on their way home. But when the soldiers discover that the bird is crippled, they abandon her, saying, as did Redden's critics,

> What have we here? A crippled bird that tries to sing? Such a thing was never heard of before. It is impossible for her to sing correctly under such circumstances and we were certainly mistaken in thinking that there was anything in such songs. Our ears have deceived us.[3]

Any reader will agree that a crippled wing has nothing to do with a bird's ability to sing. Yet many will pause before applying this same logic to deafness and poetry. Even some Deaf poets themselves were plagued by doubts about their ability to write poetry, or at least "good" poetry that would be respected in the mainstream. Such doubts were, and still are, linked with *audism*, that is, the belief—imposed by hearing society and internalized by many Deaf people—that people with "hearing loss" are inferior. One such troubled poet, Howard L. Terry, wrote in the foreword to his 1929 book *Sung in Silence*, "In offering these poems to the public I feel as if I were throwing a snowball into a red-hot furnace!"[4] Terry anticipated that he would not find many appreciative readers because his poems savored of old formalism. In defense, Terry explained what he thought was the problem of the Deaf poet.

> Deafness retards daily mental growth. The deaf man slowly falls behind his hearing brother. He moves with the slower shore current, while his fortunate brother is hurrying along with the stronger, middle current. . . . Equally gifted, the hearing poet is doing better work at thirty-five than the deaf poet. Beyond that age the

deaf writer does less work than the other; he has lost his grip, he is growing less sure of his way as times change, and he is less able to grasp and comprehend the new order of things.[5]

In contrast, many Deaf poets valued their deafness. They had long known that there was something beyond sound from which they could create poetry. Indeed, since the middle of the nineteenth century, almost every other book in English produced by a deaf poet, culturally Deaf or no, quotes John Keats: "Heard melodies are sweet, but those unheard / Are sweeter . . . "[6] But Deaf poets differed in what they took this to mean. For some, especially those who were not born deaf and experienced tinnitus, unheard melodies were the inner music in their heads. Robert F. Panara prefaced his collection *On His Deafness and Other Melodies Unheard* with "On 'Tinnitus' (Instead of a Prologue)," in which he wrote,

> I learned to count the blessing of deafness in still another way. This came with the discovery of Poetry and the realization that, at last, I had found that elusive nymph whose magic seemed to transcend that of her sister muse of song. Under her spell, the inner noises experienced a fine "sea change / Into something rich and strange" . . . Often, I would leave off writing a poem because I was overly absorbed with the melody I had conceived. . . . Sometimes . . . these improvised melodies were so haunting that I would spend the whole night sleepless and find a better balance between a certain point and counterpoint.[7]

Other Deaf poets had an understanding of unheard melodies wholly separate from sound, real or simulated. Deaf poet Earl Sollenberger, who wrote a poem called "Keats" in which he expressed his surprise at the fact that Keats was not deaf, believed visual experiences were equal to auditory ones in value. He presented both elements in his poem "Birds Will Sing" (1937), not surprisingly with the Keats quote as preamble.

> To a thrush on a mulberry bough,
> Once on a time God said:

"Sing, little fellow, sing
A sweet tune for that girl there
On the lawn.
She is watching, she is waiting,
She is listening, listening, listening."

The bird sang.

At the end God said:

"That was a good song. My choir
Back home was listening in,
And I think that We
Shall have better music from now on.
That girl there
Couldn't hear you,
But she is satisfied too."[8]

When free verse came into vogue, many Deaf poets were relieved. Free verse was more than literal to them, it was physical; it freed them from rhyming dictionaries, syllable counting, and artificial pronunciation. Some continued to write formal verse but as a matter of choice. Despite the changing poetic forms, the twentieth century did not bring full liberation for the Deaf poet. The perception that sound is the elixir of poetry persisted, and the little publicity Deaf poets received continued to be more about the idea of the Deaf poet than the poetry at hand.

That Deaf people can write is obvious, as is the power of the written word in poetry. So why should Deaf poets still be considered a novelty? It is because of the belief that Deaf poets are always missing something vital. The physical voice is popularly thought to hold a higher place in poetry than the written word. Many hearing poets subscribe to this belief. Two examples will serve to illustrate this. Here is the French poet, Jules Supervielle:

The printed matter that one follows with one's eyes, the silent and unmediated communion between the mute text and the reader, facilitate an unequalled concentration, the more precious because it opens up into an exaltation without witnesses. But isn't poetry made above all for the vocal life? Isn't it waiting for the human voice to release it from the characters of the printing press, from their weight, their silence, their prison, from their seeming indifference?[9]

Edward Hirsch agrees:

Poetry is a voicing, a calling forth. . . . The words are waiting to be vocalized. The greatest poets have always recognized the oral dimensions of their medium. . . . Writing is not speech. It is graphic inscription, it is visual emblem, it is a chain of signs on the page. Nonetheless: "I made it out of a mouthful of air," W. B. Yeats boasted in an early poem. As, indeed, he did. As every poet does.[10]

Not every poet. Deaf poets have increasingly protested against such sentiments. Ironically, they can point to the same hearing poets for thoughts about how poetry goes beyond sound—"Poetry is a soul-making activity"[11] (Hirsch) and "It is a question of inclining the heart more than the ear"[12] (Supervielle). The hearing poets' statements about the sacredness of the vocal life may be only lip service, but it affects how Deaf poets are understood, or misunderstood, as they continue to write poetry, often as a political weapon.

For more than three centuries, the Deaf world has built a cultural perspective to contravene the formidable medical perspective of deafness that brands it as a disability. Indeed, the sixteenth-century deaf French poets Pierre de Ronsard and Joachim Du Bellay, even though they did not belong to a signing community, opened the poetical record on deafness by the deaf when they dedicated poems to each other reflecting on their deafness, and they did so in remarkably positive terms for their times. In his 1548 "Hymn on Deafness," Du Bellay wrote, "I will say that to be deaf—for those who know / The difference between good and evil (they are few) / Is not an evil, only seems to be so."

Much of Deaf poetry, even by deaf poets who do not consider themselves culturally Deaf, celebrates deafness as part of the human condition—different, perhaps, but still normal and equal. Moreover, their work is a collective subversion of the sound—or, to them, unsound—theory of poetry. Breaking the most ground are the Deaf poets who do not write. After all, writing is not native to Deaf culture as is signing. They make poetry out of handfuls of air; their lexicon is cinematic, giving rise to a new poetics. One fascinating advantage of signed poetry is that it offers, as Jim Cohn declared, "an even more open field for direct treatment of the object than English-speaking poets ever dreamed."[13]

Other poets work with both written and signed languages, with a full range of pidgin and experimental work on and off the page, opening boundaries between languages. The late Deaf poet Dorothy Miles wrote in the introduction to her 1976 collection *Gestures: Poetry in American Sign Language* (book and video) that, with certain poems, she had "tried to blend words with sign-language as closely as lyrics and tunes are blended in song." She continued, "In such poems, the signs I chose are a vital part of the total effect, and to understand my intention the poem should be seen as well as read."[14]

While audism, both in society and in poetics, continues, it is provoking stronger and truer responses from Deaf poets. Contemporary Deaf poet Pamela Wright-Meinhardt was inspired to write "A Letter to C.F." after her hearing professor, in his opening lecture for a Shakespeare course, proclaimed that he pitied deaf people because they could not appreciate "the beauty of language" without hearing the dramatic voice. Wright-Meinhardt's missive in answer conveys what many contemporary Deaf poets feel.

> Art starts in the heart and is meant to touch hearts. It is folly to think, then, that not being able to hear prevents a person from being inspired by sounds. The organ of the ear is a small compartment of a whole, not the whole of a person. Millions of nerves race through a body; what's to say a few in the ear destroy a person's ability to understand music? Or poetry? Or simply to have their hearts touched? And if the message is acoustic, is it always missed? Absolutely not.[15]

Deaf poets have come a long way, but this should not come as a surprise nor a "wondrous irony."[16] Sound is but one of many vehicles through which poetry can travel from feeling and thought to expression and understanding. In other words, sound is mere medium, not source. What is often forgotten is that the human capacity for experience does not wait for sensations, but it reaches out and fills itself to overflowing. Deafness can, and does, enhance the possibilities of poetry because it compels the poet, as it did Beethoven in music, to traverse roads less traveled yet toward the same destination, the destiny of all art. The work of Deaf poets serves as a prism through which Deaf people can know themselves better and through which the rest of the world can see life in a new light.

Notes

1. John Carlin, quoted in Harry G. Lang and Bonnie Meath-Lang, *Deaf Persons in the Arts and Sciences: A Biographical Dictionary* (Westport, CT: Greenwood Press, 1995), 68.

2. Luzerne Rae, "The Poetry of the Deaf and Dumb," *American Annals of the Deaf and Dumb* 1, no. 1 (October 1847): 14.

3. Laura Redden Searing, "The Realm of Singing," in *Sweet Bells Jangled: Laura Redden Searing: A Deaf Poet Restored*, ed. Judy Yaeger Jones and Jane E. Vallier (Washington, DC: Gallaudet University Press, 2003), 208.

4. Howard Terry, foreword to *Sung in Silence: Selected Poems* (Los Angeles: Terry, 1929).

5. Ibid.

6. John Keats, "Ode on a Grecian Urn," in *The Oxford Book of English Verse, 1250–1900*, chosen and edited by A. T. Quiller-Couch (Oxford: Clarendon, 1919).

7. Robert F. Panara, *On His Deafness and Other Melodies Unheard* (Rochester, NY: Deaf Life Press, 1997), 12.

8. Earl Sollenberger, *Along With Me* (Paterson, NJ: Gayren Press, 1937).

9. Jules Supervielle, *Selected Poems and Reflections on the Art of Poetry*, trans. George Bogin (New York: Sun, 1985).

10. Edward Hirsch, *How to Read a Poem: And Fall in Love with Poetry* (New York: Harcourt, 1999).

11. Ibid.

12. Supervielle, *Selected Poems*.

13. Jim Cohn, *Sign Mind: Studies in American Sign Language Poetics* (Boulder, CO: Museum of American Poetics Publications).

14. Dorothy Miles, *Gestures: Poetry in Sign Language* (Northridge, CA: Joyce Motion Picture Co., 1976), 5.

15. Pamela Wright-Meinhardt, "A Letter to C.F.," in *The Deaf Way II Anthology: A Literary Collection by Deaf and Hard of Hearing Writers*, ed. Tonya Stremlau (Washington, DC: Gallaudet University Press, 2002), 139.

16. Ilya Kaminsky, *Dancing in Odessa: Poems* (Dorset, VT: Tupelo Press, 2004), book jacket.

John R. Burnet
(1808–1874)

DEAF HISTORY is a story of cultural warfare, but before the heavy blows comes diplomacy. "Emma," John R. Burnet's 1835 narrative poem, is a prime example of pandering to a hearing audience. It is an elaborate advertisement for "institutions for the instruction of the Deaf and Dumb." Burnet appeals to philanthropists' Christianity by describing deafness in the darkest language before outlining what schools can do for Deaf children and, implicit in this, how Deaf children are capable of learning.

We know Burnet's purpose because Emma is such a poster girl as well as her widowed mother's only joy. This dramatizes Emma's illness and subsequent deafness and her mother's agonizing over sending her to the "asylum." Emma is restored to her mother after five "brief" years, Burnet writes reassuringly. "Emma" is an illuminating historical document because the writer is patently conscious of his readers' likely attitudes toward Deaf education, then only eighteen years an institution in America.

John Robertson Burnet was born in New Jersey and grew up on his grandparents' farm. He was deafened at eight by fever. He never attended school but had some tutoring from his sister. Although he knew the two-handed British manual alphabet, he did not encounter sign language until he was twenty-one. Curious about other deaf people, he visited and was impressed by the New York Institution for the Instruction of the Deaf and Dumb. He was hired as a teacher there in 1831, but he left a year later for Philadelphia to work at his uncle's newspaper.

Before long, Burnet returned to New York to write the first comprehensive text on deafness and Deaf education in America. Published in 1835, *Tales of the Deaf and Dumb, with Miscellaneous Poems* also contained the first work of fiction by a Deaf American, a story not unlike "Emma" featuring an orphan girl. The book sold well enough for him to clear his grandfather's debts and assume control of the farm. In 1839, he married Phebe Osborn, a graduate of the New York Institution, and they adopted a hearing daughter. Burnet continued to write, but he gave up farming in 1868 and took a clerical job. A few years later, he went back to teach at the New York Institution. In 1871, Burnet received an honorary degree from the National Deaf-Mute College (now Gallaudet University).

Emma

The Deaf and Dumb! is there another word
By which more sad emotions can be stirr'd?
Speech—hearing reft! how lightly falls the weight
Balanc'd with that, of common strokes of fate,
As captives suff'd but to gaze afar
On that bright joyous world they must not share,
Gaze but to turn with desolating chill,—
And feel the dungeon darker,—colder still;
Such was the lot the deaf and dumb have borne;—
Theirs was the night that never knew a morn,—
Theirs was the dungeon dim and chill, whose gate
Was barr'd forever by remorseless fate.
Yet light to theirs the captive's transient doom,
Theirs was a deeper—more enduring gloom.
What are the body's chains to bonds that bind
The ever restless and immortal mind?
What is the darkness of the dungeon's walls
To the deep night that the mute's soul enthralls;—
Whose spell blights all affection's budding flow'rs,
And paralyzes the mind's finest pow'rs?

Could all the mutes far scattered through our land,
Be congregrated in one silent band;—
Six thousand minds in intellectual night,—
Even in this land of science's boasted light!
Six thousand souls—unknowing of a God,
Even in Christianity's most bless'd abode!
Six thousand hearts—by undeserved doom,
Lock'd up to brood in solitary gloom!
Smother'd—not quench'd,—the soul's eternal fires;
Link'd with the brutes its joys—not its desires;
(Desires but given to be still repress'd,
And smother'd, but to canker in the breast.)

Were such a band before the eye array'd,
Scarce human though in God's own image made,—
How would the heart shrink from the mighty sum,
And bleed to contemplate the deaf and dumb!

And shall the feeling in mere pity end?
Will you not too a helping hand extend?
Philanthropists,—whose kinding bosoms throb,
To spread the light of knowledge round the Globe,
Before whose far pervading,—heav'nly ray
Ye hope to see man's misery melt away;
When *reason's* hand shall lop each wild excess,
And *her* light guide the world to happiness;
Look on the deaf and dumb in your own land;
What ignorance can more your zeal demand?
What savages with minds more all debas'd?
Their hearts a wild uncultivated waste,
Whose soil's own richness prompts the growth of weeds,
And passion in unprun'd luxuriance breeds;
To lift the savage to the rank of man
And cultivate the moral wild, what plan,—
Philanthropists,—that e'er was yet display'd,
More merited from you applause and aid?

CHRISTIANS,—to whom the gospel has been given,
Glad tidings to each creature under heaven;
With this command, "Go through the world, and preach
My gospel, and to keep my statutes teach."
Do your hearts burn till on each heathen land
The gospel shine?—Does this divine command
Knock at your hearts, and urge you to fulfil,
With all your feeble pow'rs, your Maker's will?
Look on your native land,—how many rest
In more than heathen darkness, on its breast.
Aye,—in this land, where frequent temples rise,
And faithful ministers point to the skies;

Where many a circle meets for household pray'r,
That purest of all worship,—even there
Are those to whom,—though they may bend the knee,
That worship is a hidden mystery.
And shall it still be so; will you not lend
Your aid to those, who seek that veil to rend,
That shuts out from th' unhappy deaf and dumb
The prospect of a better world to come?

    Blessed by thy memory, great, good De l'Epée!*
And blessed forever that auspicious day,
When the mute sisters waken'd in thy breast,
The godlike pity that would never rest;
But, burning on through life in that pure heart,
Urg'd on thy giant mind to rend apart—
Gigantic task! the iron bands, that bound,
Ever since time began his weary round,
Thousands,—nay, millions, heaven born minds to keep
Of ignorance the lowest—darkest deep,
Where prejudice clinch'd fast the chains of fate,
And barr'd their dungeon with a mountain's weight;
Thou com'st! the mountain's weight is roll'd away,
The dungeon is unbarr'd, the chains give way,
And thy hands lead the rescu'd captives forth
To light and life and happiness on earth;
Nay more,—thou sett'st their footsteps in the road
Which leads them to their father and their God!

    Nor small the gratitude, nor mean the praise
Due to Philanthropists of later days,
Who, fir'd with kindred zeal, his steps pursu'd,
And made more straight and plain the path he hew'd.

---

* Charles-Michel de l'Epée (1712-1789) founded in Paris the first school for the Deaf and was the first teacher to use sign language for instruction.

And THOU! who saidst, *"The deaf shall hear the word,"**
O aid their efforts, till each heart be stirr'd,
Each hand impell'd to aid the glorious plan—
That seeks to lift them to the rank of man;
Nay more, to fit them for eternity,
To point their eyes, and lead their feet to thee:
From my heart's inmost depth comes forth the pray'r,
Half their lot's bitterness 'twas mine to share;
And my heart's dearest wish is still to see
That light dawn on them all which dawn'd on me.

    We cannot bid the long seal'd ears unclose,
Nor give the nerves to thrill when music flows;
To feel the power of eloquence and song
That sweep each passion in wild tide along;—
Or thrill to the heart's inmost care, to hear
Love's soft low accents murmur'd in the ear;—
Seal'd must the ears remain, and tied the tongue,
Amidst the social ring, the list'ning throng;
Seal'd to the strian that bids the grove rejoice,—
To the kind accents of a mother's voice.
Seal'd to the call that warns of dangers nigh,
To each sweet and each solemn sound beneath the sky
But we can sweeten their unhappy lot,
Yea—till its bitterness be half forgot.
Yes—we can give the longing mind to know,
And bid the spirit soar, the bosom grow,—
And the soul look, with eyes of heavenly faith,
To hope that glimmers through the gloom of death!
Yes—of this smitten, once degraded race,
Hundreds,—but late their friends' grief and disgrace
From an Asylum for the deaf and dumb,
After a few brief years returning home,
To their glad friends, the world, and in a word,

---

* Isaiah 29:18.

In mind and feelings, to *themselves* restor'd;—
Have liv'd their families' pride and ornament;
Happy,—esteem'd,—lov'd,—useful, and content,
And some a parent's part have well supplied,
And many with a christian's hope have died!

* * * * * * *

    Fair as an opening flow'r young Emma smil'd,
Her widow'd mother's joy,—her only child,
And like a twining vine she grew, and wound
Still more and more that mother's heart around.
E'en now she feels that flame immortal glow
That prompts th' unquenchable desire to know,—
The mind already claps its wings for flight,—
And thrills the heart with ever new delight;
Delight that gushes from a thousand springs,—
Sweet flow'rs,—sweet fruits,—sweet sounds,—and pretty things.
But still, of all the play things she possess'd,
She thought her bird the prettiest and best;
And she would sit and listen to its lay,
Unheeding of her kitten's frolic play;
And she would leave fruits, flow'rs, and ev'n *its* song
To drink in knowledge from her mother's tongue,
And her heart glows beneath that mother's care
With each pure feeling that makes childhood fair.
And even now her knees have learn'd to bend,
And from her lips a lisping pray'r t' ascend.

* * * * * * *

    The scene is changed, and in the widow's cot,
Her Emma's prattle, laugh, and song are not;
Her little voice in pray'r no more is heard,
His sweetest lays unheeded tunes her bird.
Has fate torn from the bleeding breast the fair
And cherish'd flow'r that grew and rooted there,

And all the mother's hopes, by that stern doom,
Sepulchr'd in the silence of the tomb?
Her hopes are buried, but her child survives,
Her own mind's breathing supulchre she lives.
Disease has clos'd the passages of sound,—
And silence cast her deep'ning spell around,
That *her* unanswer'd prattle—day by day,—
Still'd—till the pow'r of utt'rance pass'd away;
And chill'd her once warm bosom's gen'rous fire,
Making the heart within itself retire,—
Its throbs as by an incubus repress'd,
Till each once gushing feeling of her breast
Flow'd back, and stagnated upon the heart
To selfishness that lov'd to gorge apart,
And sullenness that sat in silence sour,
Shun'd company, and mop'd away each hour;
Her soul, by the reaction, crush'd downmore
Than if it ne'er had learn'd to glow or soar.
Where are her dawning intellectual pow'rs,
That knowledge suck'd as bees suck sweets from flow'rs?
Seal'd in the cells of thought, by fate's stern doom,
They sleep as sleep those bees through winter's gloom,
Waiting till spring, returning warm and bright,
Recall to life, and brace their wings for flight.
Spring to the bees, and to their flow'rs shall come;
But when shall spring come to the Deaf and Dumb!
Oh with what agony the mother press'd
Her silence stricken offspring to her breast,
And tried each remedy, but tried in vain,—
To call back the departed sense again.
Slow to believe, she must believe at last
That the irrevocable doom was past,
That lock'd up all enjoyment's purest springs,
And clog'd forever the mind's flutt'ring wings.
But—as the mother bird, whose new fledg'd care
Chain'd to the ground by cruel school boy's snare,
Essay in vain on flutt'ring wings to soar,—

But cherishes her helpless offspring more;
So with increasing love, the mother smil'd
Through bitter tears, upon her silent child,
And Emma, as she felt the warm embrace,
And the hot tear that fell on her own face,
Felt her heart glow with thoughts not all forgot,
And wonder'd why her mother wept, and yet spoke not.

* * * * * *

Years pass;—another change comes o'er the scene,
Emma has reach'd the period of fourteen;
And she has all forgot that once she heard,—
Or, if the memory be sometimes stirr'd,
Tis but the shadowy outline of a dream,
Or as the moon beam on the troubl'd stream.
Her soul has learn'd to bear up against fate,
And feels more lightly the accustom'd weight.
And the first torpor of the long stunn'd mind
Has pass'd,—but left a galling chain behind.

Her form is budding into womanhood,
How her cheek mantles with the crimson flood?
How her eyes sparkles with the fire within!
What grace in all her actions, all her mien!
Each outward charm has nature made her dow'r
That warms the heart of man to passion's pow'r,
Nay more,—has in that peerless form enshrined
A priceless heart,—a highly gifted mind.
And,—as the mother watch'd each op'ning grace,
What bitter feelings in her breast had place,
To think so sweet a flower unseen must bloom,—
And that rare mind be shrouded in a living tomb.

But that heart's longings are not all in vain
To share with kindred hearts its joy or pain,
Nor,—to perpetual winter though condemn'd,—

Will its warm flow so near its spring be stem'd.
And as th' unfailing brook,—its wonted tide
Dam'd up,—but overflows on every side,
So when the mind's accustom'd channels close,
Through gestures, face, and eyes it overflows.
How her soul flashes from that restless eye,
Whose glances speak its immortality,
Striving to pierce the mystery that shrouds
All things beyond th' unaided sense in clouds!
How flies her mind, with painful impotence,
To each remaining avenue of sense;
Grasping with eager and tenacious hold,
The scanty knowledge that chance may unfold?
Her pow'rs still struggling with elastic bound
Against the weight that drags them to the ground!

So the cag'd bird,—suspended in a grove
Where all around is harmony and love,
Condemn'd to see,—and seeing,—not to share
The soft endearments of each happy pair,
As its gaze follows that far darting flight
That field and mead and forest to the sight
With all their myst'ries,—all their charms,—reveals;—
How does it long to join those airy wheels!
How does it long to pierce the shade, whose bound
Has limited its vision's restless round!
To look through nature with admiring eye,
And soar on fearless wings into the sky!
And with unquench'd—unquenchable desires,—
It vainly flutters round, and beats against the wires.—
His heart to all fine feelings dead and cold
Must be,—who could the captive's doom behold,
Nor long to set the struggling pris'ner free,—
Or,—at the least,—soothe its stern destiny.

And all who saw pitied the mute,—and some
Told that to educate the deaf and dumb

The effort had been made; nor vainly made;
And favor'd too by legislative aid;
That Emma might, to an asylum sent,—
Be there supported by the Government.
Yet shrunk instinctively the mother's heart
Nor from her helpless—only child would part,—
And must the child, o'er whom she watch'd so long
With love that her misfortune made more strong,
Leave the fond guarding arms around her twin'd,—
To the cold hand of strangers be consign'd,
And years apart from that lone mother live?
How cruel seemed the dread alternative.—
But must her Emma's gifted heart and mind
To everlasting darkness be resign'd,
Must joy's best fountains never be unseal'd
Nor the rich stores of knowledge be reveal'd,
Must her immortal mind be doom'd to grope,
Without one hand to guide, one heavenward hope,
One intellectual ray to gild the gloom,
Through life's dark vale of tears to the dark tomb?
It is enough, the weeping mother said,
Each selfish feeling shall aside be laid.
How hard the task! But Emma we will part,
My love itself shall tear thee from my heart!

* * * * * *

The scene is chang'd—An edifice I see,
A noble monument of charity,—
That near the new world's great commercial mart,
In its unostentatious grandeur tow'rs apart.
I see an hundred of the deaf and dumb,—
Collected from full many a distant home,—
Within this noble pile,—whose walls—to them
Open'd another world,—a fairy realm;
A realm of a new language,—all their own,
Where mind was visible,—and knowledge shone,

As the bright all revealing daylight shines
To the poor native of Cracovia's mines,*
When, first emerging from his regions dim,
The broad,—bright world above seems heaven to him.
And there is a fair girl, whose eyes seem red,—
Nor yet the tears are dry so lately shed—
Sad had been Emma's parting hour,—and when
She saw strange faces all around her,—then
Her heart shrunk back with desolating chill,
Nor, for a time, would its wild throb be still.
But round her kind hearts from kind faces beam'd,
And the soul's sunshine on her spirit gleam'd,
That melted all her doubts and fears away,
As morning fogs fade in the blaze of day.
Soon her once cag'd and insulated mind
Rejoices in communion with its kind.
She *now* no longer feels herself alone,
Her knowledge but what could be glean'd by one.
But the mind's commerce, *here* set free from thrall,—
Makes each one's store become the wealth of all,
Here, from the speaking limbs, and face divine,
At nature's bidding, thoughts and feelings shine,
That in thin air no more her sense elude,—
Each understands,—by each is understood.
Here can each feeling gush forth, unrepressed,
To mix with feelings of a kindred breast.
Here does her teacher's skilful hand unroll
The curtain that hung round her darken'd soul,—
Revealing all the secret springs that move
The once mysterious scene, around, above,
Here, when the sense is pall'd,—she learnst enjoy
And revel in delights that never cloy.—
To spurn this clog of clay and wander free

---

* In the original publication, Burnet added the following note : "In the salt mine of Cracow in Poland, it is said, many persons have been born and passed all their lives without ever seeing the light of day."

Through distant ages,—o'er far land and sea.
Collecting, one by one, each precious gem
That decks of science the bright diadem.
Till her mind,—rev'ling in the stores of thought,—
Ceases, almost, to murmur at its lot!
Nay more—her teacher,—pointing to the skies,—
Unrolls the sacred volume to her eyes,—
The charter of her immortality,
That teaches how to live, and how to die;—
Bids virtue lean on him who died to save,—
And look from earthly woes beyond the grave!
      Lo! in those walls a congregation met,
A hundred mutes in silent order set,—
A congregation met for praise or pray'r,
And yet no voice,—no song,—no sound is there.
Yet not from the heart's thoughts ascends alone
That pray'r or praise to heavenly mercy's throne;
The teacher stands, to pray or teach, and all
The eyes around drink in the thoughts that fall,
Not from the breathing lips,—and tuneful tongue,—
But from the hand with graceful gesture flung.
The feelings that burn deep in his own breast
Ask not the aid of words to touch the rest;
But from his speaking limbs, and changing face,—
In all the thousand forms of motion's grace,
Mind emanates, in coruscations, fraught
With all the thousand varied shades of thought.
Not in a cloak of words obscur'd, confined—
Here free conceptions flash from mind to mind,
Where'er they fall their own bright hues impart,—
And glow,—reflected back—from ev'ry heart!

* * * * * *

      Five happy years in this Asylum past,
And each year seem'd more happy than the last;
For,—as the miser brooding o'er his store,—

The more he has but hugs and hoards it more,
So Emma, since her thoughts first learn'd to glow,
The more she knew, but long'd the more to know.
Or, as the hero, when one world was won,—
Sigh'd, till another's conquest was begun;—
So Emma, while, to her enraptur'd gaze
Science her rich and boundless realms displays,
Feels, as each realm is conquer'd and possess'd,—
The thirst of knowledge strengthen in her breast.
And, to her entrance day she oft looks back,
As a bright dawning in life's darken'd track;—
A glorious dawn of mental, heavenly light
Upon a mind that long had grop'd in night.
And, wer't not that her mother's letters spake
Of things that kept remembrance still awake,
All that had pass'd ere *then* might almost seem
But the dim recollection of a dream.
And on the bustling world she looks afar,
As one might look upon a distant star,
Throughout whose vast and fruitful zones each field,
By the opticians wondrous skill reveal'd,
(If ever human skill might mount so high
The secrets of another world to spy.)
A race like ours gives to our wond'ring gaze,
Their toil, their strife, their changing fate displays.—
We see their millions struggling on through life
For fame, or gold;—and wonder at their strife.
What was the world to her?—the wells that bound
Her feet,—but give her mind an ample round,—
Where *light* the slower pace of *sound* supplies,
And carries all thought's errands to the eyes;
Those walls contain'd her world, and there content,
Had fate allow'd, she could her life have spent.
But her five years are pass'd, the time has come
When she must leave this long lov'd foster home.
Though to a mother's arms returning, yet
She could not leave those walls without regret.

And she, the mother, who so well had prov'd
By parting with her child how much she lov'd;
For that child's sake self doom'd to solitude
Through five long years of cheerless widowhood,
As her recover'd daughter to her heart
She press'd, and felt they were not more to part,
And gaz'd upon that lovely form and grace;
And day by day was more surpris'd to find
Still more expanded Emma's heart and mind;
She felt her painful self-denial *then*
Had been an hundred fold repaid again.
                    Cetera desunt.

James Nack
(1809–1879)

SCARCELY A DECADE passed between the founding of the first permanent American Deaf school and the publication in 1827 of the first book by a Deaf American. *The Legend of the Rocks, and Other Poems* contains sixty-eight poems composed before James Nack was eighteen years old. His long, lyrical poem "The Minstrel Boy" opens with doleful words about the state of the uneducated and unsaved Deaf, a sentiment that Nack's future friend John R. Burnet replicated in the opening of his poem "Emma."

Later in the poem, Nack writes about what is really on his mind. He alternates between describing consolations—in beauty, art, nature, and poetry—and lamenting his fate, despairing of ever gaining "fame, fortune, independence," and "the apple smile of love"—things that Deaf people did not quite yet think they deserved. Nack's anxieties are soothed by looking forward to the Hereafter, where he imagines he will find the things that were beyond his grasp on Earth as a Deaf person. He moved beyond this fatalism in his later work. He is assertive in his short poem "The Music of Beauty," in which he declares, "I pity those who think they pity me."

James Nack was born in New York City to a poor family. Homeschooled by his older sister, Nack could read by age four. When he was eight, he stumbled down a staircase and hit his head against a fire screen. He came out of his weeks-long coma to find himself deaf. In 1818, Nack enrolled at the newly opened New York Institution for the Instruction of the Deaf and Dumb. By the time he left school four years later, he had written many poems, including a complete tragedy. One of his poems so impressed Abraham Asten, a city clerk, that he helped Nack obtain a job in a lawyer's office. The lawyer's library enabled him to continue his education and to teach himself foreign languages. Asten also put Nack in touch with writers who encouraged him to publish a collection of his verse. *The Legend of the Rocks, and Other Poems* received considerable praise, which was heightened by the critics' amazement at his youth and deafness. They held up Nack as proof of the success and necessity of Deaf education.

Nack married a hearing woman in 1838, and they had three daughters. He worked as a legal clerk for over three decades and published three more volumes of poetry, verse dramas, and short prose pieces.

From The Minstrel Boy[*]

[...]

Unheard, unheeded are the lips by me,
　　To others that unfold some heav'n-born art;—
And melody—Oh dearest melody!
　　How had thine accents, thrilling to my heart,
Awaken'd all its strings to sympathy,
　　Bidding the spirit at thy magic start!
How had my heart responsive to the strain,
Throb'd in love's wild delight, or soothing pain!

In vain—alas, in vain! thy numbers roll—
　　Within my heart no echo they inspire;
Though form'd by nature in thy sweet control
　　To melt with tenderness, or glow with fire,
Misfortune clos'd the portals of the soul,
　　And till an Orpheus rise to sweep the lyre
That can to animation kindle stone,
To me thy thrilling power must be unknown.

Yet not that every portal of the mind
　　Is clos'd against me, I my lot deplore;
Although debar'd by destiny unkind
　　From one that never shall be open'd more,

---

[*] Nack prefaced the poem with the following note, referring to himself in the third person, "The very thoughts which were passing in the mind of the author, at the time of writing the 'Minstrel Boy,' are undisputedly exprest in that Poem; and more freely, perhaps, than they would have been, had he expected that the effusions of his pen would be exposed to the public eye; which he could not imagine, at a time that there was not even one well informed person, to whom his poetical pretensions were known. However, he submits it as it is to the public, as none of his friends have advised the suppression of any part; but not without some apprehension that some passages may be construed as expressive of impatience under the dispensations of heaven, as at the time of writing it, he was peculiarly unhappy, and too deficient in submission to, and confidence in, his Creator."

Still from my lot at times relief I find,
    When science, I thy temple stand before,
Whose portal thou hast open'd, to my sight;
The gems displaying there enshrin'd in light.

Blest Science! but for thee what were I now?
    Denied the rights of man, as to employ
Those rights incapable—mankind, if thou
    Hadst not aris'n the barrier to destroy,
No human blessings would to me allow;
    The sensual pleasures which the brutes enjoy
Alone were mine, than brutes a nobler name
Entitled only by my form to claim!

Friends of misfortune's race, whose heart and hand
    Are never clos'd against affliction's prayer,
To heathens can your charity expand!
    Will you to them the gospel tidings bear?
And yet neglect your own, your native land?
    O shall the gospel be a stranger there?
Behold the Deaf and Dumb! What heathens need
More eloquently for your aid can plead?

Strangers to God!—And shall they still be so?
    Will you not lift a hand the veil to rend—
Their intellectual eyes to heaven throw,
    And lead them to a father and a friend?
Will you not snatch them from the gulfs of woe,
    To which they else unrescued must descend?
O save them! save them! that the Deaf and Dumb
May bless you in this world, and in the world to come!

Spirit of philanthropy! thou hast smil'd
    Where the attempt already has been made,
To cultivate the mind's deserted wild;
    Though eloquence were pow'rless to persuade,
None can compare the unenlighten'd child

With those who have already known thine aid.
But in a difference so wide must feel
A deep, an irresistible appeal.

None can behold how eagerly they cling
 Around the new creator of their mind,
Who, the Prometheus of the anxious ring,
 The hallow'd flame in learning's fane enshrin'd
Kindles within them, yet refuse to bring
 Where they with these may equal blessings find,
The numbers who unaided still demand
Those blessings from a benefactor's hand.

Neglect you will not suffer to efface
 The work that your benevolence began;
Nor bid them grovel still in thraldom base,
 Who claim from you the faculties of man;
You will not if you love the human race,
 You will not, cannot, for no christian can,
In whom the God of christians has imprest
This truth,—in blessing we indeed are blest!

Would that of eloquence I own'd the might,
 To paint the feelings in my breast enshrin'd,
For those enwrapt in the Cimmerian night
 Whose darkness had encanopied my mind,
If Science on me had not stream'd her light,
 And rais'd me to a level with mankind!
When I my happier lot with their's compare,
Can I to feel or plead for them forbear?

Of life to cheer my desolated scene,
 The rays of friendship beam but for a while;
"Like angel visits few and far between,"
 Are those my dreary moments that beguile;
And oft, alas, misfortunes intervene,

To tear me from a friend's endearing smile;
But e'en in solitude the cultur'd mind
Society within itself can find.

The works of genius lying at my side,
    I claim in each an ever welcome friend,
From whose society, whate'er betide,
    Misfortunes have no power my mind to rend;
On whom, when human intercourse denied,
    I may for rational delight depend;
And till these eyes are clos'd in endless night,
I cannot be bereft of that delight.

Shall I of utter loneliness repine,
    While I with a delighted eye can see
The spirit of genius, breathing in the line
    That kindles with its wild sublimity,
While beauty dazzles in the lay divine,
    And pathos melts the soul to sympathy,
And fancy wafts my thoughts upon her pinions,
Roving the fairy land of her dominions?

To me, when beauty's fingers lightly tread
    The quiv'ring strings, no rapture they impart;
Yet, melody, though to thine accents dead,
    Whose witchery had else subdu'd my heart,
From infancy my spirit has been led
    In blissful thraldom by thy sister art;
Sweet poetry! still it shall own thy sway,
Till on the wings of death it soars away.

[. . .]

Perhaps unhonour'd I must live and die,
    And when the Minstrel Boy is swept away,
His harp within his grave unreck'd shall lie,

And with his name become oblivion's prey;—
Well, be it so—I care not if no eye
    But thine, shall ever dwell upon my lay,
Should thine embalm these pages with a tear
For him, who had but thee to value here.

O but for thee, the hour that I was born
    I oft had curs'd, to agony consign'd,
When from my brow the wreath of health was torn,
    And pain a thorny coronet entwin'd;
When writh'd my spirit proud beneath the scorn
    Unmerited, of the ignobler mind;
Or when the demon Hope some bliss pourtray'd,
In laughing mockery to see it fade.

[. . .]

Despair is no deceiver—ev'ry ill
    It throws before anticipation's view,
The hour of destiny I find fulfil;
    While all that might have blest in being true,
Has prov'd a falsehood, and a mock'ry still;
    Then henceforth what have I with Hope to do,
But curse each past, and fly each future spell,
That only dawns in heav'n to set in hell?

And let me then despair—despair of all
    Fame, fortune, independence, might bestow,
Or from the angel smile of love might fall;
    My doom is fix'd to be a wild of woe!
A doom that heaven never shall recall,
    Till I am rescued from this world below;—
And then—does Hope again deceive in this?—
I—even I—may know a ray of bliss.

[. . .]

And none are more exquisitely awake
        To nature's loveliness, than those who feel
The inspiration of the muse;—who take
        From her the glowing thoughts that as they steal
Around the soul entranc'd, a goddess make
        Of nature, to whose shrine of beauty kneel
The fond enthusiasts, adoring all
Within her we may dread or lovely call.

[. . .]

Earth! thou art fair and glorious, but all
        Thy beauty and thy glory are a shade,
That low beneath the hand of time must fall:—
        And Woman! must thou too in dust be laid?
Ah no! the beauteous fetters that enthral
        Thy spirit, only are decreed to fade;
That spirit, on a seraph's glowing wing,
From earth shall to its native heaven spring.

Thine earthly shrine is but thy prison—still
        Such loveliness is flung around thee here,
That as it beams before mine eyes, they fill
        At times, unbidden, with the tremulous tear,
And though my bosom shoots a painful thrill
        To think that aught so beautiful—so dear—
Should to the hand of death resign its bloom,
A trophy to enwreath around the tomb!

Must all then know corruption?—even thou,
        My angel girl—my dear—my blue-ey'd maid!
Shall those bright eyes that smile upon me now,
        Resign the beams that oft have on me play'd
So tenderly? Shall reptiles kiss thy brow,
        Enwreath'd among the tresses, that to shade
Thy beauteous lineaments around them dance,
Veiling thy loveliness which they enhance!

O blinded Infidel! whoe'er thou art—
　　If thou canst be an Infidel *indeed*,
Love's flame must be extinguish'd from thy heart,
　　Or love itself would turn thee from thy creed—
To thy belov'd would eloquence impart
　　Against a fate so horrible to plead
As thou wouldst pass on them, and all mankind—
Annihilation in the grave to find!

The soft confession trembling on the tongue
　　Of beauty, when replying to thy flame—
The cherub infant, that around thee clung,
　　With innocent fondness, lisps a father's name—
The friend whose heart in unison is strung
　　With thine, resigning to affection's claim
Each secret of his bosom—are they thine?—
The joys that are not—never shall be mine?

What rapture in my heart is ever glowing,
　　When one I meet who to that heart is dear,
A smile of tenderness upon me throwing,
　　Although his voice shall never reach mine ear!
But thou—the music of affection, flowing
　　From lips belov'd, who art allow'd to hear,
Since more than me affection thee doth bless,
Shall thy devotion to her sway be less?

Around me when those darling children cling,
　　Belov'd as they were mine—when on my knee
They prattle, and my heart unconscious wring
　　With the fond accents, that if heard by me,
As they believe!—My tears resistless spring
　　To think how blest I were, if that might be
Which never shall be!—While by them carest
With all a father's love they animate my breast.

And sure no father with an infant pair
    So lovely—so belov'd—could cast his eye
Upon th' angelic beauty which they wear,
    Yet say that they were born alone to die—
O no! around them there is thrown an air
    Breathing of heav'n and immortality,
In accents, that to marble hearts appealing,
Would melt them with the eloquence of feeling.

It were a deed of mercy in the sire
    His babe to strangle, when it first appears
In being, to preserve it from the ire
    Of stern misfortune, through this vale of tears
Who follows all, if in the grave expire
    The spirit's consciousness—for nothing cheers
The darkness of our lot, when Hope denies
Her radiant star—the beacon of the skies!

To live is to be wretched—and to die
    To part with all we love—and O! forever!
Our only hope our dust may mingling lie
    Where death itself shall want the power to sever;
But shall their smiles again address our eye,
    To kindle recapture there? O! never, never!
Is this thy faith? Art thou so blest in this,
That thou canst mock the Christian's dream of bliss?

[. . .]

Say, Atheist, hast thou ever gaz'd upon
    The loveliness of death, when on the bier
Reclin'd th' inanimate pale form of one
    Who living lov'd thee, and to thee was dear?
O! sure while such a scene beholding, none
    Could say, "All that remains of thee is here;
And all that to thy form its value gave,
Must with it be extinguish'd in the grave!"

O! if thy faith were mine, and if the doom
　　Were past upon me—(Never may it be!)—
The lovely—the angelic girl, to whom
　　This heart is giv'n, bereft of life to see,
What should forbid me then upon her tomb
　　To end my being and my misery?
The deed Religion's voice forbids alone,—
By those unreck'd who dare her truth disown.

[. . .]

My blue-ey'd maid! when bending at the shrine
　　Of heav'n, thy name is wafted in my prayer;
The dearest hope avow'd to heav'n is thine,
　　That we may meet with one another there;
And if on earth to ever call thee mine
　　Be rapture that to know I must despair,
I in the blissful hope can be resign'd
That we shall in eternity be join'd.

[. . .]

Thy voice angelical with mine to blend,
　　In unison adoring heaven's King;
Together at the throne of God to bend,
　　While angels are around us hovering,
The fervent prayers that from our hearts ascend
　　To waft above the sky upon their wing,—
If aught might be in terrestrial bliss,
To be compar'd with heav'nly, it were this.

[. . .]

O! dream of bliss! like every other dream
　　Of bliss that I have cherish'd, if it fade;
Should fortune never throw so bright a beam
　　Upon a lot so long enwrapt in shade;

If thou canst but return me thine esteem
    For all my love to thee, my blue-ey'd maid!
If one prefer'd above me shall command
What I may seek in vain—thy heart and hand!

Whoever he may be who thus shall blight
    The dearest hopes that can inspire my breast,
On him nor thee may aught of evil light,
    But may you be in one another blest
As I would have been with thee, if I might
    Have won the angel bride by him possest;
And heard from thy dear lips the music breathe
Of love, entwining there his blissful wreath.

[. . .]

"I love thee!"—Worlds on worlds if they were mine,
    To buy those accents should away be thrown;
All other melody I could resign,
    Might I but hear those tender words alone
Warbling upon those rosy lips of thine,
    My blue-ey'd maid, where music might enthrone
Her sweetest magic—oft repinings rise
To think that even this my lot denies.

Yet why repine against the will of heaven,
    By erring man so little understood?
Misfortunes may be found in mercy given
    To work together for our final good;
And all the blessings that from me are riven
    Evils might have accompanied, that would
Upon my lot far heavier have weigh'd
Than those upon me that shall now be laid.

Thy will, my God! Thy will be done, not mine,
    For all by Thee is order'd for the best;
Myself, mine all, I to Thy hands resign;

I ask but that my lov'd ones may be blest
Here and hereafter, and with me may join
    In an eternity of joy and rest,
With cherubim and seraphim to bend
Before our God—our Father—and our Friend.

The fetters of the ear shall be unbound,
    And silence shall no more the lips enthral,
When the Archangel's awful trump shall sound,
    Death from its sleep awakening—when all
Shall at its summons burst the trumbling ground,
    With myriad voice replying to his call,
In shouts of ecstasy, or shrieks of fear,
Before the bar of heaven to appear.

And then, my blue-ey'd maid, may we unite
    With all we love below, to hymn the praise
Of our Redeemer—O with what delight
    Shall I inhale the music of thy lays,
Warbling with those of cherubim, while bright
    Eternal glories clothe us in the blaze
That emanates from Mercy's smiling eye,
Hov'ring the throne of the Almighty nigh!

[…]

The Music of Beauty

To me thy lips are mute, but when I gaze
Upon thee in thy perfect loveliness,—
No trait that should not be—no lineament
To jar with the exquisite harmony
Of Beauty's music, breathing to the eyes,
I pity those who think they pity me;
Who drink the tide that gushes from thy lips
Unconscious of its sweets, as if they were
E'en as I am—and turn their marble eyes
Upon thy loveliness, without the thrill
That maddens me with joy's delirium.

John Carlin
(1813–1891)

JOHN CARLIN is a baffling question mark in the history of Deaf leaders. He was a successful artist, was responsible for great strides in organizing Deaf people, and, as his lovely writing attests, was an embodiment of English literacy through a sign-based education. Yet he supported oralism, the method by which deaf children are taught to speak and read lips, and he seems to have harbored some bitterness about his deafness for all of his long and illustrious life. Ironically, this may have been because he wanted very much to write poetry; never mind that he did and was widely acclaimed and published. He, however, did not feel that he could write "proper verse." One wonders if he would have felt better if the standard rules of versification in his day were not so tightly regulated.

Carlin's insecurities about his writing notwithstanding, he labored over his poems, and "The Mute's Lament" is a credit to his efforts. It is a catalog of lovely sounds that Carlin "hears not," and it ends with his hope for becoming hearing and able to speak in heaven. The poem is contradictory in that most of the things he regrets not hearing are also visual, and Carlin describes them in visual terms, but he is ultimately disappointed in his being deaf to these sounds.

Other Deaf poets followed Carlin and Nack in writing of becoming hearing in heaven, but this viewpoint grew to be increasingly unacceptable to the cultural discourse of Deaf Americans. Angeline Fuller Fischer writes in her 1883 poem "Closing Hymn for the Sunday Services of a Deaf-Mute Convention" of Deaf people's ears unstopping and their tongues unloosing in heaven, but she asks God to hear their "voiceless song" of praise, for Him to accept sign language. Breaking away from this entirely, an anonymous poet wrote a piece virtually opposite of "The Mute's Lament" called "The Sign-Language of Heaven," in which only visual things are described and credited as God's signing. This last poem was published in 1891, the year Carlin died.

John Carlin was born deaf to a poor Philadelphia cobbler. As a child, he roamed the city with a group of deaf street urchins who eventually came under the care and instruction of the crockery merchant David Seixas. This "school" became the Pennsylvania Institution for the Deaf, from which Carlin graduated in 1825. He apprenticed himself to several artists and even studied painting in Europe from 1838 to 1841. When Carlin returned to the United States, he established a studio, where he painted miniature portraits on ivory. In 1843, he married Mary Wayland, an alumna of the New York Institution, with whom he had five children.

Carlin was deeply involved in the signing community. He wrote about its issues, raised funds for the first Deaf church in America and a home for elderly Deaf people, and founded the Manhattan Literary Association of the Deaf, the first of its kind. An accomplished signing stylist, he gave the main address at the opening of the National Deaf-Mute College in 1864. During the commencement ceremony, the college awarded its first honorary degree to Carlin. After the advent of photography, Carlin turned to painting landscapes; he wrote extensively on Deaf-related and mainstream topics and, in 1868, he published a children's book, *The Scratchsides Family*.

The Mute's Lament

I move—a silent exile on this earth;
As in his dreary cell one doomed for life,
My tongue is mute, and closed ears heedeth not,
No gleam of hope this darkened mind assures
That the blest power of speech shall e'er be known.
Murmuring gaily o'er their pebbly beds,
The limpid streamlets as they onward flow
Through verdant meadows and responding woodlands,
Vocal with merry tones—*I hear them not.*
The linnet's dulcet tone; the robin's strain;
The whippowil's; the lightsome mockbird's cry,
When merrily from branch to branch they skip,
Flap their blithe wings, and o'er the tranquil air,
Diffuse their melodies—*I hear them not.*
The touches—lyric of the lute divine,
Obedient to the rise, the cadence soft,
And the deep pause of maiden's pensive song,
While swells her heart with love's elated life,
Draw forth its mellow tones—*I hear them not.*
Deep silence o'er all, and all seems lifeless;
The orator's exciting strains the crowd
Enraptur'd hear, while meteor-like his wit
Illuminates the dark abyss of mind—
Alone left in the dark—*I hear them not.*
While solemn stillness reigns in sacred walls,
Devotion high and awe profound prevail,
The balmy words of God's own messenger
Excite to love, and troubled spirits soothe—
Religion's dew-drops bright—*I feel them not.*
From wearied search through long and cheerless ways
For faithless fortune, I, lorn, homeward turn;
And must this thankless tongue refuse to breathe
The blest word "Mother," when that being dear

I meet with steps elastic, full of joy,
And all the fibres of this heart suspective
Throb with Nature's strongest, purest love?
Or, that this tongue must still forbear to sing
The hymn sublime in praise of God on high;
Whilst solemnly the organ peals forth praises,
Inspired and deep, with sweetest harmony!
Though sad and heavy is the fate I bear,
And I may sometimes wail my solitude,
Yet, oh! how precious the endowments He,
T'alleviate, hath lavished, and shall I
Thankless return his kindness by laments?
O, Hope! How sweetly smileth Heavenly Hope
On the sad-drooping soul and trembling heart!
Bright as the morning star when night recedes,
His genial smile this longing soul assures
That when it leaves this sphere replete with woes,
For Paradise replete with purest joys,
My ears shall be unsealed, and I shall hear;
My tongue shall be unbound, and I shall speak,
And happy with the angels sing forever!

Mary Toles Peet
(1836–1901)

JOHN CARLIN AND James Nack were among the first students to attend their respective schools for the Deaf, and their educational experiences were fundamentally different from that of Mary Toles Peet and succeeding generations of Deaf school alumni. While the first wave of Deaf teachers, who were the peers of Carlin and Nack, did not have role models, they became the mentors of Peet and her counterparts. By the time Peet entered the New York Institution, the influence of Deaf leaders and the signing community on the education of Deaf children had gone well beyond that of Laurent Clerc, the first Deaf teacher in America.

The sentiment running through Peet's poetry is conclusive evidence of this positive influence. "Silence is sweeter than sound" is the message shared by all of her poems presented here. "Thoughts on Music" is Peet's response to hearing people's misguided sympathy; "To a Bride" finds her reminding a Deaf friend of the same point; and "The Silent Child of Art" assures the reader that deafness is a boon to an artist.

Mary Toles Peet was born in Green, Pennsylvania, but her childhood was spent in Arkwright, New York. She attended a district school until contracting brain fever and becoming deaf at thirteen. Two years later, she enrolled at the New York Institution for the Deaf and Dumb, where one of her teachers was Isaac Lewis Peet. He fell in love with his pupil but did not confess it until shortly before her graduation in 1853. A year later, they married and eventually had several sons and a daughter, Elizabeth.

Because of her husband's role as principal of the school, Mary served as the unofficial head matron. She also taught various classes whenever a teacher was needed to fill a temporary vacancy. Most of her poems are occasional verse, commissioned by friends for events, and many of them appeared in the *American Annals of the Deaf*. Peet suffered a stroke in 1891, just a few years after her husband's death. For the remainder of her life, she lived with or near her daughter, and she spent her last years living on the campus of Gallaudet College, where Elizabeth worked. Elizabeth published a collection of Peet's verses soon after her mother's death.

Thoughts on Music

They tell me oft of the witching song
    That thrills the list'ner's heart,
And of the soft melody
    Breathed forth with music's art:
They tell me, too, of the joyous strain,
    Which bursts with magic power,
From the heart where love and hope have laid
    Their brightly woven dower.

And then they tell of the sounds which come
    Afar from the sea's deep caves,
Of the voice of the wind which sighs among
    Old Ocean's towering waves;
And the wild, deep music, which comes up
    From the breakers' dashing roar
And the storm cloud's voice, when, as in wrath,
    His torrents madly pour.

And they tell me, too, of the wild bird's song
    Afar in the green woods dim,
And of the lark's glad trill, which seems
    Of praise a heartfelt hymn,
And that the feathered sprites at which
    I sit and gaze each day,
Send forth to the still heavens, as well,
    Their soft, melodious lay.

And then they tell of the sounds which come
    From the battlefield afar,
Of the thrilling peal of the "trump and drum,"
    And the martial strains of war;
Then turn from these to tell sweet tales,
    Of the evening zephyr's notes,

And all the varied melody
    Which round them ever floats.

Then I gaze into their faces, and see
    The smile no longer there,
And they grieve that never unto me
    May float, on the stilly air,
One sound of this glorious minstrelsy,
    One echo of the voice
Which swells through Nature's thousand tones,
    Making all earth rejoice.

Yet deem not, since I am debarred
    From all the melodies of sound,
Earth has no music for my heart,
    Nor that my soul is bound
By that dull seal which has been placed
    Upon my outer sense,
For the music of my inward ear
    Brings joy far more intense.

To a Bride

Thou askest, O my friend, a song to-day;
But what soft note, what subtle melody
Can thy young heart's delicious joy convey?

In Life's enchanted lyre, one chord alone
Can thrill thee with a music all its own,
And fill thine heart with one most perfect tone.

What need, then, hast thou that I sing to thee?
June roses for thy bridal, fair to see,
Are sweeter music than my notes can be;

And song-birds flitting thro' the fragrant air,
And stars that gleam, like living eyes, from where
Thine own turn softly in thy troth-plight prayer.

Then silence, sweeter than all varied sound,
Shall fold thee soft, like loving arms around,
For life's most perfect gift thy heart hath found.

The Silent Child of Art

[Written on the graduation of Miss Ella Dillingham, a young art student at the New York Institution.]

From out the south a gentle wind
    Blew o'er me as I slept,
And, fair and bright in my girlish dreams,
    A radiant Presence stepped
Before my eyes. Oh the look benign
    That o'er her fair face played
Was tender as my mother's touch,
    While calm for me she prayed!

This Presence, so divinely fair,
    Bent with a queenly grace,
The moonlight making bright her hair,
    The spirit light her face;
And with a sign she beckoned me
    To follow where she led;
Then I, not knowing yet her name,
    Arose with wavering tread;

When all along the path she went
    Sprang flowers of varied hue,
Some with the sunshine were besprent,
    And some were wet with dew,
And forms of wondrous grace uprose,
    As if to meet her smile,
And slow and stately was her step,—
    I following all the while.

Then with a look whose meaning since
    Fills all my waking years,
She pointed to the seven fair hills
    Whereon Art's shrine appears.

Oh, tender as the kiss of love
　　Upon a weary brow,
Beamed upon me her divinest smile
　　As lowly I did bow.

For then I knew her name was Art,
　　And she had chosen me,
From out the silence where I dwelt,
　　Her humble child to be.
And evermore with reverent soul
　　I follow her behest,
And day by day her hidden truths
　　I seek with tireless quest.

For somewhere in the coming years,
　　O Rome! fair home of Art,
Her hand shall open wide thy doors
　　And joy sing in my heart;
For form and color then shall fill
　　With music all my days,
And e'en this silence shall become
　　More sweet than shouts of praise.

Laura C. Redden
(1840–1923)

ONLY A VERY FEW Deaf people have made writing their vocation, and Laura Redden is among the most successful of them. Because of societal bias against women in the professions, she wrote many of her poems and articles, which were published in the most popular magazines, under the name Howard Glyndon. She holds the distinction of being the only Deaf person to have a town named in her honor—Glyndon, Minnesota.

Since Redden treated much of her work as merchandise to be sold for mass consumption, she did not often write on deafness. When she did, however, she created a valuable allegory (*The Realm of Singing*) and several poems that stand as classic examples of two genres found in scores of other poems by Deaf poets. "My Story" is a lamentation on deafness, and "Thomas Hopkins Gallaudet" is dedicatory verse that celebrates teachers of the Deaf.* While "Thomas Hopkins Gallaudet" is perfectly commercial, the lamentation in "My Story" may have held genuine meaning for Redden, who had to cope with becoming deaf at age eleven instead of in early childhood. But the poem distinguishes itself in that she saw beyond her grief at her loss, realizing that it could hardly compare to the troubles in the world around her.

---

* Thomas Hopkins Gallaudet (1787–1851), with Laurent Clerc, founded the first permanent school for the Deaf in America. Redden's poem recounts the terrible lot of Deaf people before Gallaudet came along and lifted them up. Gallaudet became the most frequently celebrated figure in nineteenth-century Deaf America, and he was frequently described as the savior of Deaf people. Harlan Lane has likened Gallaudet to Abraham Lincoln in that Lincoln was the most important figure in black history until the black community's discourse became strong enough to put black figures in his stead. Later in the twentieth century, when Deaf people gained more access to their history, Laurent Clerc, the Deaf counterpart to Gallaudet, gradually gained ground and replaced Gallaudet as the savior figure.

Laura Catherine Redden began her writing career while a student at the Missouri School for the Deaf, where she enrolled four years after spinal meningitis rendered her deaf in 1851. Soon after graduating in 1858, Redden served as a columnist and editor of a church newspaper. In the tense political climate leading up to the Civil War, she decided to work as a journalist rather than marry a Presbyterian minister to whom she was twice engaged. *The St. Louis Republican* sent her to Washington, D.C., as a war correspondent. By writing notes back and forth, she interviewed many notable subjects, including Abraham Lincoln, and published a collection of short biographies of members of the House of Representatives. In 1864, Redden published a collection of her war poems on the subscription plan. In 1865 she embarked on a long sojourn in Europe, during which she continued to write for American newspapers.

Upon her return, Redden found a job in New York City at the *Evening Mail*, published widely in leading magazines, and, in 1873, published another volume of poetry, *Sounds from Secret Chambers*. She married Edward Searing, a lawyer, and they had a daughter, Elsa. Because of health concerns and because the marriage was not working, Laura and Elsa moved to California. In 1921, to resurrect her mother's literary reputation, Elsa assembled a collection of Redden's work as *Echoes of Other Days*.

My Story

Brave, generous soul! I grasp the hand
    Which instinct teaches me is true;
This were indeed a royal world,
    If all were like to you!

You know my story. In my youth
    The hand of God fell heavily
Upon me,—and I knew my life
    From thence must silent be.

I think my will was broken then,—
    The proud, high spirit, tamed by pain;
And so the griefs of later days
    Cannot distract my brain.

But my poor life, so silence-bound,
    Reached blindly out its helpless hands,
Craving the love and tenderness
    Which every soul demands.

I learned to read in every face
    The deep emotions of the heart;
For Nature to the stricken one
    Had given this simple art.

The world of sound was not for me;
    But then I sought in friendly eyes
A soothing for my bitter logs,
    When memories would rise.

And I was happy as a child,
    If I could read a friendly thought
In the warm sunshine of a face,
    The which my trust had wrought.

But then, at last, they bade me hope,
    They told me all might yet be well;
Oh! the wild war of joy and fear,
    I have not strength to tell!

Oh, heavier fell the shadow then
    And thick the darkness on my brain,
When hope forever fled my heart,
    And left me only pain.

But when we hope not we are calm,
    And I shall learn to bear my cross,
And God, in some mysterious way,
    Will recompense this loss.

And every throb of spirit-pain
    Shall help to sanctify my soul,
Shall set a brightness on my brow,
    And harmonize my whole!

By suffering weakened, still I stand
    In patient waiting for the peace
Which cometh on the Future's wing,
    I wait for God's release!

A nation's tears! A nation's pain!
    The record of a nation's loss!
My God! forgive me if I groan
    Beneath my lighter cross!

Henceforth, thou dear, bereaved land!
    I keep with thee thy vigil-night;
My prayers, my tears, are all for thee,
    God and the deathless Right!

Thomas Hopkins Gallaudet[*]

The mandate, "Go where glory waits,"
    Was less than naught to him:
He sought the souls whose day was dark,
    Whose eyes, with tears, were dim.

As yet his glory rests secure
    In many a grateful mind,
First blessed by him, with knowledge sweet,
    And linked into its kind.

They lay in prison, speechless, poor,
    Unhearing, thralls of Fate,
Until he came, and said "Come out!
    It is not yet too late!"

He came, and lifted up, and spoke;
    He set them in the sun.
The great work goes on and on
    That was by him begun.

And in this bronze he lives again,
    But more within each heart.
To which he said, "Be of good cheer,
    Let loneliness depart."

We lift the veil, and see how Art
    Has fixed his likeness there,
And placed beside him one whose life
    He lifted from despair.[†]

[*] Thomas Hopkins Gallaudet (1787–1851), with Laurent Clerc, founded the first permanent school for the Deaf in America, the American School for the Deaf.

[†] Alice Cogswell (1805–1830) was the first student at the American School for the Deaf. She was the daughter of Mason Fitch Cogswell, who hired Thomas Hopkins Gallaudet to learn about education of the Deaf in Europe. Gallaudet returned with Laurent Clerc, a Deaf teacher from the school in Paris.

She stands there as the type of those
    To whom he gave his all;
Those sorrows touched him till his love
    Went out beyond recall!

Ah, well it was, that little fight
    Was fostered by the Lord!
Ah, well it was, he loved the child
    And felt her fate was hard!

Ah, well it was, he turned himself
    Unto that speechless woe,
Which made the world a lonely road
    One hundred years ago!

Rest here, thou semblance of our Friend,
    The while the world goes by!
Rest here, upon our College green
    Beneath the bending sky!

Remain, and bless the chosen work
    That found its source in thee—
'Tis through thy love that ye, thy sons,
    Are happy, strong, and free.

Rest here, Father of us all!
    And when we pass thee by,
'Twill be with bared head and heart,
    And mutely reverent eye.

Thank God, He gave thee unto us
    To free us from our woe,
And put the key into thy hand
    One hundred years ago.

Angeline Fuller Fischer (1841–1925)

WHAT THE SIGNING community in the nineteenth century knew of its history was limited to the Bible, the founding in Paris of the first school for the Deaf, and the saga of how Thomas Hopkins Gallaudet and Laurent Clerc began the education of the Deaf in America in Hartford, Connecticut. This wispy past did not stop Deaf people from cultivating what most cultures enjoy—a creation story. Angeline Fuller Fischer's "Scenes in the History of the Deaf and Dumb" has all the trappings of what was and would be told and performed in Deaf schools and clubs generation after generation, with little, if any, variation; that is, how deaf people were "considered brainless, soulless, useless things" before education of the Deaf was born.

"To a Deaf-Mute Lady" is about the special bond between Deaf people who share things in common in addition to being Deaf. The signing community has always been a small world, but in the days when travel was slow, Deaf meetings were especially cherished events. Deaf people could not afford to be selective about their friends, but the Deaf experience created a link strong enough to overcome most, though not all, of mainstream society's prejudices regarding gender, class, race, and education. Fischer's poem appears to be dedicated to a Deaf woman with whom she connected on an even deeper level, giving her the occasion to write "spirits grow / By slow degrees, yet ever quickly note / Affinity, wherever it exists."

Angeline Fuller Fischer was born in Savanna, Illinois. She attended a local school until whooping cough and typhoid deafened her in 1854. For the next five years she floundered, unable to continue her education, until she learned about the Illinois School for the Deaf. Fischer enrolled in the school, but because of recurring blindness, she left two years later.

Beginning in 1875, Fischer became active in the signing community, doing volunteer work, teaching, and writing. By 1880, she was the leading Deaf feminist; she pushed for women's participation in the first National Association of the Deaf conference. At the conference, she met George Fischer, the Deaf editor of a mainstream county newspaper in Maine, and they married in 1887. She published a collection of poems called *The Venture* in 1883.

Scenes in the History of the Deaf and Dumb

Scene First.

> Behold a miracle! a bush on fire,
>> Burning intensely, burning unconsumed,
> Note how the flames rise higher and yet higher,
>> And all the air around is high perfumed,
> With odors richer far than any flower
>> Exhales at day's first dawning, when the Sun
> Drinks up the dew-drops and goes forth in power,
>> His daily journey leisurely to run,
> To carry from the land of song and star
>> Brightness and warmth into the west afar.

> Note further that each wave of perfumed light
>> Shimmers and shines as tho' the sun and moon
> And all the stars of heaven, most fair and bright
>> With all their force of midnight and of noon,
> Were multiplied ten thousand thousand times,
>> And then ten thousand times ten thousand more,
> Until the number aggregates or climbs
>> Past computation's limit, mete or score;
> Aye, multiplied so brightly that it seems
>> Earth's every jewel in one casket gleams.

> Well may the air be sweet, well may it shine
>> With wondrous radiance, such as was not seen
> Ever before, for power we know DIVINE
>> Has touched that bush, erewhile so low, so mean,
> A common thing, from which each passing brute
>> Might browse at pleasure, or by well-aimed blow
> Break, nevermore to leaf or bloom or fruit,
>> Or thrive beneath the sun's most genial glow,
> A bush to be, by any strong man doomed,
>> Uprooted, or by common fire consumed.

And see, near this vast pile of earth and rock
    Known as Mount Horeb, Moses wends his way
Intent upon the pasture of his flock,
    Intent on keeping evil beast at bay,
Thinking, perchance, of Egypt and the sin
    Of sore oppression he had witnessed there,
Until his soul revolted, and from kin
    He fled, unable more to see or bear,
Fled all alone, in horror and in grief,
    To find with strangers comfort and relief.

Behold his wonder when at first the sight
    So wholly marv'lous, so paralled,
That it would fill a common soul with fright,
    And even him in speechless wonder held
For a brief while, then shaking off all fear,
    Of harm and danger, he right bravely cries,
"Not burnt, strange, very strange, I will draw near
    To see this fire which flickers not nor dies,
But blazes on, surpassing everything
    Of which historians talk or poets sing."

But harken now, for scarcely has his word
    Of firm decision echoed on the air,
Or his broad breast, within so deeply stirred,
    Drawn breath, more of the thrilling sight to bear,
When from the bush there emanates a sound,
    A voice that thrills him to his being's core,
And bends his soul in homage more profound
    Than any voice had ever done before,
As it commanded, "Nay, do not draw near,
    Take off thy shoes, the ground is holy here."

Having responded promptly to his name
    In the brave words of Abraham, "Here am I,"
And bared his feet before the curious flame
    Which while it rose so brilliantly, so high,

Made the whole plain a consecrated place
    Henceforth, forevermore, while time endures,
A spot historian's pen would sometimes trace,
    And venturous trav'lers visit in their tours,
A spot to prove till earth and time shall end
    That our Creator also is our friend.

Fitting it was the astonished man should hide
    His face in awe and listen in a maze
Of humble, solemn joy that he, denied
    Awhile the right to walk earth's peopled ways,
Might in the lonely desert meet his Lord,
    And learn from His own lips that He gave heed
To all His children's wrongs, and would accord
    Judgment to their oppressors, and would lead
Them forth in triumph to a better land,
    Where peace and plenty smile on every hand.

'Twas further fitting that he should reply:
    "I hear Thy words, and I would gladly go
Unto Thy people, who in anguish cry,
    Yea, I to them Thy promises would show,
But who am I, to that I should be so blest,
    So honored? Thou hast others fitter far
To lead Thy children to their longed-for rest,
    Send them to be a guide, a morning star,
To those to whom Thy pledge was long since given
    Of Thy best favors granted this side Heaven.

"Yea, I would gladly go, but much I fear
    That tho' they long have prayed, are praying now,
For a deliverer, or for hope to cheer
    Their hearts, until it please Thee to allow
Their servitude so very long and great
    Entirely and forevermore to cease,
And lead them forth unto their own estate,
    Their promised land of liberty and peace,

Me for their leader they will not receive,
    Nor that Thou sendest me at all believe."

Quickly the Lord whose glory made the place
    So wonderful, made answer: "Do not fear
To do my bidding, I will give thee grace
    For all the way that seems so long and drear.
Haste, bravely haste upon thine honored way,
    Bid the proud tyrant set my people free,
Go without fear of evil night or day,
    For I—certainly I—will go with thee,
To end the long, dark night of cruel woe,
    And to their rest my chosen people show."

Meekly again the favored man replied:
    "I am not eloquent, but slow of speech,
Is there no other better qualified
    Thy chosen people to lead forth and teach?
I have no lack of love for Thine nor Thee,
    But he should have the power quickly to sway
The people's minds who dares a guide to be,
    Or Thy commands before them seeks to lay;
And since my speech is poor, my tongue is slow,
    Choose a more fitting guide, and bid him go."

Brighter, far brighter then, glowed the strange fire,
    Shimmered more grandly, every twig and leaf—
Higher the flames rose upward, and yet higher;
    A pause ensued—a silence deep, but brief—
And then the Lord by questions made reply:
    "Who made man's mouth? *who made the deaf and dumb*?
Say, did not I, the Lord? and cannot I
    In any time of need bid words to come?
Fear not, for surely I will go with thee,
    I, the I AM, thy help, thy guide will be.

"But since thou art so diffident, so meek,
    Behold thy brother, Aaron, he shall be
To thee a mouth, and through him thou shalt speak
    Whatever I communicate to thee.
Fear neither king nor people, Lo! the rod
    Thou holdest now, and even thine own hand
Shall henceforth be a sign that I, the God
    Of Abraham, Isaac, Jacob, all, command,
Anoint, appoint and full commission thee
    To lead my captives forth to liberty."

Scene Second.

Right well the Promiser His promise kept,
    And with wise words in every hour of need,
Filled each old prophet's mouth, and Israel slept
    Or waked or journeyed, as His word decreed,
Until at last they gained the promised land,
    And safely dwelt, blessing and being blest,
Till, seeing they to evil gave a hand,
    Affliction entered, their faith to test,
And teach that God is ever watching near,
    And notes all lack of love or trust or fear.

Then when they cried for help, wise prophets came,
    Telling them of a time, a happy day,
When by repentance they again could claim
    Much they possessed before they went astray,
Saying the lame should sometime nimbly leap,
    The blind should see with strong and perfect eyes,
The deaf hear plainly, and joy yet more deep,
    The dumb, no longer dumb, return replies,
And every age should know and should declare,
    God for the suffering has a special care.

And while the years went by, the wondrous years,
    Working their changes great and manifold,

Men nursed high hopes, or sadly talked of fears,
 Prayed, toiled and strove for bread, for land and gold,
And as their fancy or their means decreed,
 They builded temples in which Science, Art,
Religion, Learning, each could garner seed,
 Of which all devotees could take a part,
And carry forth to strew with generous hand,
 Broadcast, to bless and beautify the land.

Aye, more, they builded Homes, wherein the lame,
 The sick, the weak, could find a place of rest,
When those who were their friends only in name,
 Forsook them, left them helpless and distressed;
Homes, into which the suffering ones could go,
 Until the storm of trouble could pass by,
Or they could drink their mingled cup of woe,
 And calmly, quietly lie down to die.
Aye, for all such every enlightened age
 Left a fair record upon historic page.

But tho' the Lord so plainly had declared
 That He, himself had made the deaf and dumb,
And had His word of honor pledged, He cared
 For each, for all of them, and gave them some
Portion and share and interest due, and claim,
 In every right or privilege of the age,
In which they lived, rights dear even in name,
 Alike to the uncultured and the sage—
Aye, gave them of all these a liberal share,
 And cared for them with loving father care.

They were passed by, neglected, doomed to scorn,
 Considered brainless, soulless, useless things,
Men even cursed the house where such were born,
 And wounded them with worse than scorpion stings;
Grudged them their food, even grudged them light and air,

And took their life, without regret or shame,
As if their cry for help—their dying prayer
        For justice could not—would not—have a claim
In Heaven's high courts, as if the Lord had not
        Vowed care for them, or had His vow forgot.

Scene Third.

Haste with me now across the bridge that spans
        The gulf of centuries and with me behold
Another miracle, angelic bands
        Filling the eastern horizon, their harps of gold
Echoing the sweet music, and they sing
        A song ne'er heard by sin-marked men before—
O, blessed song—earth has at last a King—
        "Peace and good will!" Hate, give thy warfare oe'r;
Man need no longer live to sin a slave—
        IMMANUAL comes to mediate and save.

Proper it was, a new, a brilliant star
        Should rise upon that blessed, blessed morn—
Rise to proclaim to earth both near and far,
        The glorious tidings that at last was born
The true Messiah, who would break the night—
        The long, dark night of fear which sin had wrought,
Bring immortality and Heaven to light,
        By pure, redeeming love, passing all thought,
In measure so immense, no word but so
        Its height nor depth, length nor breadth can show.

A king who comes in pride and pomp to reign
        May look unpityingly on others' grief,
And leave the sufferers to endure their pain
        Till in death's slumbers they can find relief;
But He, the King of Glory, could not go
        Past suffering thus, His mission was to heal
Whom sin had wounded, and by deeds to show

Where'er He went since He might not conceal
That in the form of weak humanity
He held the power of true divinity.

Therefore he helped the weak—the hungry fed,—
Let palsied captives from their bondage go—
He healed the sick—called back to life the dead,
And bade the mourners' tears no longer flow;
He touched blind eyes, and lo! they clearly see;
He said Ephphatha to the lips long dumb,
Applied to silent ears the mystic key
Of firm command, and bade sweet echoes come,
Then left the happy throngs their joy to tell
In grateful praise—"He doeth all things well."

O, favored eyes, that opening to the light
Looked first upon their Saviour; doubly dear,
O, favored ears, that waking from a night
Of utter silence, first of sounds could hear
The Master's voice, and with the lips long dumb
Speak first to Him, and thank Him for His love,
That matchless love, which prompted Him to come
From all the glory of His home above
To take from death its sting, the grave its gloom,
And save the sinful from their righteous doom.

Scene Fourth.

Again haste with me o'er the bridge of time,
See, we stand now upon our native soil;
It is the hour for vesper bells to chime,
The hour when men can rest awhile from toil,
When children love on grassy plats to play,
See, there a group is busy at a game;
And there, apart them a little way,
Stands one who will not answer to her name,*

---

* Fuller is referring to Alice Cogswell.

However loudly they may bid her come,
　　For she, alas! is deaf—is deaf and dumb!

Has God no pity for the stricken child?
　　Does He not care that she is so alone?
Will He not heed her wish, her anxious prayer
　　Which she can utter only in a moan?
O, question not, O, question not—He cares,
　　He loves the stricken one, and even now
Counts over all her tears and voiceless prayers
　　For a deliverer, let us meekly bow,
Our heads in reverent awe and drop a tear
　　Of thankful joy that help at last is near.

She is no common-fated, short-lived one,
　　No pretty picture upon which to gaze
A little while, then toss aside or shun
　　For grander things; where'er her pathway lays
Her name in history's page henceforth will fill
　　An honored place, as sure as Justice weighs
True merit. Doubt and fear be still, be still.
　　Though nothing now the embryo fact betrays,
A grateful, happy girl is waiting here,
　　A man famous for all time is near.

And help is coming, tho' she knows it not,
　　Near by a student, weary with his book,[†]
Lays it aside and saunters to the spot,
　　Awhile upon the merry group to look;
And now his eye, his Heaven-directed eye,
　　Rests on the silent, isolated one,
Look! hark! he heaves a sympathizing sigh,
　　And questions earnestly—"Can naught be done
To set her captive thoughts and feelings free
　　And give her mind its natural liberty?"

---

† The student is Thomas Hopkins Gallaudet.

Surely an angel must have told the child
    He was no common man for her to fear;
Look, she upon her first advance has smiled,
    And shakes her head, meaning, "I can not hear,"
Alas, poor child; others can say the same,
    Like you, to Heaven for help they long have cried,
And God at last acknowledges their claim,
    And sets the door of mercy open wide;
But he who longs to teach you first must turn
    To sunny France, a method there to learn.

For there the Abbé de l'Epée waits
    To teach by graceful movements of the hands
A way which will, despite each one who prates
    Against it, break effectually the bands
Which have so long held dormant precious powers,
    And doomed full many a noble heart and mind
To idle days, to lonely wretched hours,
    To ignorance and all its ills combined,
Waits now, surrounded by a little group,
    The heralds of a vast, exultant troop.

O, blessed, truly blessed, are the hours
    When looking down upon His suffering ones,
God notes their sorrows and their fettered powers,
    Notes how against them time's strong current runs,
Notes till His father heart can bear no more,
    And cries "Enough," and bids deliverance speed
To compass land and sea, nor once give o'er
    Their searching for relief till they are freed
Who cry for help. Such hours are highly blest
    And are of gratitude the constant test.

Scene Fifth.

Love is a wondrous leveller indeed;
    The old and young turn twins at its command;
And aliens, at any time, by it decreed,

Though ears be deaf, and lips be wholly dumb,
Eyes say in tones most sweetly eloquent,
    "Fear not, sweet heart, for I will surely come,
Yes we, God willing, will clasp hands again;
    A little while our paths must lie apart,
And till I come, good-bye, fear not, sweet heart."

And though the absence be prolonged for years,
    The kind "God bless you, we again shall meet!"
The anxious, waiting heart sustains and cheers,
    While faith and hope the assuring words repeat,
And fancy, at its pleasure, gaily builds
    Air-castles most magnificently grand;
Of fond anticipation brightly gilds
    The blessed sometime, when they two shall stand
Together, who, though bound in mind and heart
    By sympathy, awhile must walk apart.

Surely, O, surely, many an angel band
    Hovered about the honored ship that bore
That noble student from his native land
    On his grand mission; surely, too, before,
Aye, with, and after him, God's blessing went;
    And he was kindly guided, day by day,
Favored and prospered, and was duly sent
    Proudly rejoicing on his homeward way,
Bringing a brother helper, 'round whose name
    Justice would sometime twin a wreath of fame.*

And just as surely angels hovered near
    That stricken girl, whose isolated state
Challenged that good man's pity, till all fear
    Of danger or of failure, small or great,

---

* Fuller is referring to Laurent Clerc, the Deaf teacher who left his native France in 1816 to become the first Deaf teacher of the Deaf in America.

Was cast aside, and very often they
    Fed her with hopes—sweet manna of the soul—
Or showed her pictures of that happy day
    When from her life the heavy cross shall roll
And she, with fervent, grateful joy elate
    Could promise others freedom yet more great.

Scene Sixth.

    A ship is slowly sailing into port,
        Fire a salute, let all the land be glad,
    Proclaim a gala day of rest and sport,
        Sing thankful songs till not a heart is sad,
    Call that poor stricken girl, a maiden now,
        Bid her with grateful kiss of welcome haste
    To meet him; bid her make a solemn vow
        Ever to keep his name in memory traced;
    Ever to honor him who holds a key
        That soon will set her captive senses free.

    Nor hers alone—give God his dues of praise,
        His mercy is not narrow in its scope,
    He sets no favored few near joy's warm blaze
        Leaving the many in cold gloom to grope,
    He hears, He heeds each dumb child's eager prayer,
        And from their lonely, isolated worlds
    Will in His own good time, with loving care,
        Gather them into safe and happy folds,
    Where signs will picture or will echo sound,
        And break their silence, partial or profound.

    O, blessed work, to break the prisoner's chains!
        O, happy task, to give the hungry food!
    O, joy untold, to ease the sufferer's pains!
        Or see that rugged paths with flowers are strewed,
    And all this blessedness was theirs who gave
        Sound to the deaf and language to the dumb;
    Who told them of the Christ that came to save,

And made them heirs of happiness to come,
This was their angel work, though hard and slow,
 And challenges respect from friend and foe.

Write, proudly write their names, Gallaudet, Clerc;
 Paint them in letters of the richest gold,
Carve them in marble, mention them in verse,
 Of grandest measure, and have often told
In prose most eloquent, how they have wrought
 Emancipation from a bondage dire,
Have given to Heaven-created will and thought
 Power to reach outward, onward and aspire,
With hopes of realization, to great heights
 Of all that here ennobles or delights.

Call them philanthropists or call them friends,
 But love and honor them forevermore,
And long as vapors rise or dew descends
 Hold blest the day they stepped upon our shore.
The ship they came in perished long ago,
 And they long since were summoned from the field
Wherein they toiled so faithfully to sow
 Seed that each year returns more bounteous yield,
And grateful reapers now throughout the land
 Gather the harvest and pronounce it grand!

Gather, then look with hopeful hearts away
 Toward the future, because teachers wait
In phalanx deep, and deepening every day,
 E'en to the borders of our mighty State;
Brave men, whose names 'tis honor to repeat;
 Fair women, wise in love's mysterious lore;
All, all great hearts, whom, though they never meet,
 They feel are friends, true to the inmost core,
Whose plea, whose boast, throughout all time to come,
 Shall rightly be, "We taught the deaf and dumb."

To a Deaf-Mute Lady

We met but once, just for a little while,
And ever since that hour, deep in my heart
Your name has lain inscribed indelibly,
And in the picture gallery of my mind
Your image has retained a worthy place,
And I will gaze upon it in the days
That yet may add unto my span of life,
My knowledge and the number of my friends.
The modest grace, the cordial sympathy
Revealed both by your countenance and words,
Roused in my heart a tender, latent chord
That then vibrated, and is vibrating
Even yet, most pleasantly.
Our meetings and our partings may be termed
A matter of small consequence, but life, you know,
Is made of little things, and spirits grow
By slow degrees, yet ever quickly note
Affinity, wherever it exists,
In any one they casually may meet,
And so it was with me that long ago
I saw in you a spirit that aspired
Above, beyond herself, and so my heart
Thrilled with a sense of true affinity,
And owns to-day that it is richer for
Those moments spent with you.

Alice Cornelia Jennings (b. 1851)

IN "A PRAYER IN SIGNS," Alice Cornelia Jennings answers any doubts, advanced by some hearing philosophers and religious leaders before and during her time, as to whether Deaf people could pray. What is more, she contends that they do so "with force more potent than the spoken word." She would have had reason to make this declaration because the Lord's Prayer was the first thing ritualized in American Sign Language. Translated in a highly stylized manner, the different versions recited in Deaf school chapels and churches outdid one another in gravity and eloquence. This exercise may have been the precursor of ASL poetry.

The signed rendering of the Lord's Prayer often was used in exhibitions promoting education of the Deaf to the public because it almost never failed to impress hearing people who had no knowledge of the language. However, the fact that audiences were well familiar with the words of the prayer probably helped people think they understood more of the signs than they actually did. While Jennings is confident that it is the signers who really know how to "lift up hands in prayer," she maintains that Deaf people are just as subject to the human condition as hearing people, saying "O hearing brother, we are like you still."

Alice Cornelia Jennings was born in Worcester, Massachusetts. She became deaf when she was eight years old. Her sister and father, a clergyman, educated her until she became one of the first pupils at the Horace Mann School for the Deaf in Boston, Massachusetts. Denied admission to Gallaudet College, which had not yet begun enrolling women, Jennings turned to the Society to Encourage Studies at Home and Chautauqua University, studying and teaching for fifteen years. Her career as a published writer began in 1871 and included at least two collections of poems, *Heart Echoes* and *My Queen*. The date of her death is uncertain, but it is known that she was living at the Riverbank Home for the Aged Deaf in 1901.

A Prayer in Signs

No uttered word is ours—no solemn tone
    The reverent air bears upward to the sky:
No eloquence of meaning, borne along
    Of voice and accent, meet the God on high.

But dare ye tell us that we do not pray—
    We who so truly "lift up hands of prayer,"
And by the speaking gesture mark the way,
    Our heart's desire would take to reach Him there?

"Our Father!" that appealing gesture lifts
    With force more potent than the spoken word,
Desire, petition for the precious gift
    Held in the hand of One All-Seeing Lord.

"In Heaven!" we picture in the circling sweep
    Of arm and hand, the glorious dome above;
"Holy Thy Name!" with reverent movement keep
    The sacred thought of purity and love.

"Thy Kingdom!" with imperial touch we show
    The badge of royalty—the sceptre's sway;
And that Thy glorious Will may work and grow
    Potent and perfect, this and every day.

Our opened hands with daily bread to fill
    The Lord we ask, "Forgive as we forgive":
O hearing brothers! we are like you still—
    The hardest this to pray, and this to live.

From tempter's touch, whene'er beside he stands—
    We pray Thee still our weakness to defend:
And by the symbol strong of broken bands
    We crave deliverance, succor, to the end.

Once more the royal sign—"Thy Kingdom Thine!"
    "The Power," that sign is vital, living, strong:
"The Glory": rays of brightness seem to shine
    And scintillate around us, sweet and long.

"Forever and forever!" round and round
    The finger sweeps, and who shall tell us then
Expression for the prayer we have not found,
    Nor join us in our glad and grand "Amen"?

George M. Teegarden
(1852–1936)

GEORGE M. TEEGARDEN was not a poet but rather a versifier who wrote in what would later be recognized as the American Victorian mode. He devoted most of his verse to excruciatingly mainstream subjects. Even when he turned to matters closer to home, he processed them in the same formal manner. Still, his poems about the National Association of the Deaf and Gallaudet College are important contributions to the historical record of the signing community.

Teegarden is the first poet in this book to have graduated from Gallaudet College. That Gallaudet is the mecca of Deaf culture is evidenced by the fact that all of the following poets, with only a few exceptions, have either studied or taught at Gallaudet. While the preceding poets in this anthology can be linked together through acquaintance—Nack, Burnet, Carlin, and Peet all knew each other, and Redden and Fischer each knew at least two of them, and so on—the convergence of Deaf students at Gallaudet makes the degrees of association even closer.

George Moredock Teegarden was born in Jefferson, Greene County, Pennsylvania, but his family moved to Iowa when he was a child. He was eleven years old and attending public school at the time he became deaf; he was then sent to the Iowa School for the Deaf. When he graduated from Gallaudet in 1876, he was invited to join the teaching staff of the newly established Western Pennsylvania School for the Deaf. Teegarden taught there for forty-eight years. During that time, he established and supervised its printing department and edited the school publication, *The Western Pennsylvanian*.

Deeply interested in teaching English literacy, he published *Different Words in Uncommon Senses* and coauthored a collection of stories adapted from classic fairy tales, fables, and mythology. This collection, *The Raindrop*, became a bestseller in the teaching field and remained in print for nearly ninety years. His school produced a book of his own stories, *Stories Old and New* (1903), all of which were written in such a way that they were highly translatable into American Sign Language. He collected most of his verse in *Vagrant Verses*, which he published privately in 1929. Teegarden and his wife had a daughter, Alice, who became a teacher at the New York School for the Deaf at White Plains.

The "Nad"*

The "Nad" is out of swaddling clothes—
He's lusty and his horn he blows,
　　　You bet.
We all will join this hustling band
　　Nor make our bow to voices "canned"—
　　　Not yet.

We like not the Procrustean bed,
Nor all with the same spoon be fed—
　　　We'll fight.
To check bad laws in this free land—
　　Stand by our cause so true and grand—
　　　Our right.

And east and west and north and south,
By every sign and word of mouth,
　　　We'll sing
The praises of the N. A. D.,
　　And put to flight the enemy,
　　　A-ling.

If you're a Nad, why, that's all right,
You're numbered with the best tonight,
　　　My son.
Are you a Nad? If not, why not?
　　Right here and now, upon the spot,
　　　Be one!

---

　* This pronoun refers to someone who is a member of the National Association of the Deaf (NAD), which was founded in 1880 and ever since has been the nation's leading advocacy organization devoted to the welfare and civil rights of Deaf people. "Are you a member of NAD?" can be signed with only two signs and an inquiring facial expression as "You NAD?" Hence, its translation back into English might be "Are you a Nad?"

Gallaudet College

(Fiftieth Anniversary)*

Hail Gallaudet! Thy sons and daughters throng
Into thy halls with laughter and with song;
In grateful homage, true, they praises bring,
And to thee, Gallaudet, in gestures sing.

Thou hast lifted aloft the cup of life,
Bubbling with hope and the strength of strife;
And they who have quaffed, shall they e'er forget
Thy most precious gifts? Hail Gallaudet!

Out of the shadows of darkest night,
From the length and breadth of this land of might,
And some have essayed the summits of fame—
Have trooped to thy fountains, the silent bands.

Many are marching o'er duty's rough road,
Thankful for sinews from Wisdom's abode;
And some have essayed the summits of fame—
Looking not backward except to thy name.

Hail, thou Gallaudet, guide of our youth,
Lead e'er thy children on to light and truth;
Thy scroll of fifty years bears naught but praise—
Shall it not last, in truth, through endless days?

A crown, Oh, Gallaudet, rests on thy brow;
Pride, Honor, Glory, Love before thee bow.
Ne'er shall thy spirit die, nor we forget—
Hail Gallaudet, thou Friend! Hail Gallaudet!

---

* The poem was written in 1914, fifty years after Abraham Lincoln signed the charter establishing the National Deaf-Mute College.

J. Schuyler Long
(1869–1933)

"I Wish That I Could Tell" is but one of many poems Deaf people have written about the music of tinnitus, the music for their eyes, and the music of signing hands. It is such a common subject that it is prevalent even in American Sign Language poetry; such classics as Ella Mae Lentz's "Eye Music" and Cara Barnett's "My Music" mirror the ideas found in the written poems. The similarities among these poems have much less to do with imitation than they do with correcting the ever-present mainstream attitude of how sad it is that Deaf people cannot hear music. Long writes in his poem that he wishes he could tell hearing people about what he enjoys, but "they would not understand." Until they do, the poem about Deaf people's music is here to stay.

Joseph Schuyler Long was born in Marshalltown, Iowa. He started to lose his hearing at age eleven, after an accident and a bout with spinal meningitis, and became totally deaf by the time he was sixteen. He graduated with the first regular class of the Iowa School for the Deaf in 1883. He attended Gallaudet College, where he was the star quarterback on the football team. After graduating, he taught at the Wisconsin School for the Deaf until 1901, when he received an invitation to become the head teacher of his alma mater. A year later, Long was appointed acting principal, a position that became permanent in 1908.

Out of the Silence, his collection of poems, appeared the same year. Long was deeply committed to the preservation of sign language against the spread of oralism as well as the maintenance of high "classical style" standards in signing. He presented widely on the subject and compiled a dictionary of signs that was published in 1909. *The Sign Language: A Manual of Signs* was the definitive textbook of its kind for four decades. In 1914, Gallaudet awarded Long an honorary doctorate in recognition of his work as teacher, editor, poet, and lexicographer.

I Wish That I Could Tell

In the sound of song and music
    There's a charm for those who hear,
And they look upon me sadly
    When they see me standing near.
And they think that I am lonely
    As they reckon what I miss,
And they seem to be so sorry
    That I lose this cherished bliss.

But I wish that I could tell them,
    As I smile and turn away,
Of the voices ever singing
    Through the night and through the day—
Voices full of sweet reminders
    Of the days of long ago,
And I hear again the echo
    Of those songs I used to know.

And I wish that I could tell them
    Of the music that I hear
With its vibrant tone resounding
    On my inner conscious ear,—
How it thrills and, creeping o'er me,
    Steals away the bitter sense
Of the wrong that Nature did me—
    This her gift in recompense.

And I wish that I could tell them
    Of the music that I see
In the buds of spring unfolding,
    And the moving melody
In the motion all about us,
    In the birds and in the flowers,

In the happy eyes of children
　　As they look their love in ours.

And I wish that I could tell them
　　Of the most delightful things
That I hear and see in silence
　　When my inner fancy sings.
And I wish that I could tell them
　　Of the music in the hand
When in song it moves in rhythm,—
　　But they would not understand.

Agatha Tiegel Hanson
(1873–1959)

TOWARD THE END OF the nineteenth century, uneasy distinctions were drawn within the Deaf community between "deaf-mutes" and "semi-mutes." The latter group tended to have more residual hearing, and the very term "semi-mute" meant they could speak to some degree, either because they had received oral training or simply had retained the skill after becoming deaf. Because the oralism movement forced people in the signing community to take a stand, such people had to choose between consciously becoming a "full mute" or shifting their identity.

The oralist philosophy espoused by Alexander Graham Bell and other hearing teachers convinced mainstream society that deaf people should use whatever hearing they had and should develop their speaking ability as much as possible. This is why Agatha Tiegel Hanson speaks of deafness as a "burden" in her poem "Semi-Mute," something that deaf-mutes definitely did not say about their deafness. Hanson's sentiments might never be justified according to the "Deaf strong," but they can be explained. She contracted spinal meningitis and became deaf at the age of seven. This was especially traumatic for her because she came from a musically inclined family and showed promise as a musician herself. And, save for two years at George M. Teegarden's Western Pennsylvania School for the Deaf, she was educated in public schools, an early and rare case of what would later be known as *mainstreaming*. That "there is no standing still" was, and is, a familiar state of mind for those who attempt to balance living between two clashing worlds.

Agatha Mary Agnes Tiegel Hanson was born in Pittsburgh, Pennsylvania. She entered the National Deaf-Mute College (Gallaudet) in 1888. She was elected the first president of O.W.L.S., today the Phi Kappa Zeta sorority at Gallaudet. Tiegel graduated first in the Class of 1893, and was the first woman to receive a bachelor's degree from Gallaudet. She then secured a teaching job at the Minnesota School for the Deaf, where she met and married fellow teacher, renowned architect, and one-time National Association of the Deaf president Olof Hanson. When Olof was ordained a minister, they moved to Seattle, Washington. Agatha's poetry and her influential essay "The Intellect of Woman" were collected and published privately by her daughters.

Semi-Mute

A river deep of silence
    E'er swells our souls around.
Its tide flows and submerges
    The weaker tide of sound.

Now memory flashes through us,
    Now lingers with us long.
Sweet strains of vanished music
    Make up its haunting song.

Yet must we bear our burden,
    Yet must we walk our way,
And slowly, surely build a work
    That will endure for aye.

We can control the future,
    Can live for well or ill.
Let us clasp hands and forward.
    There is no standing still.

James William Sowell
(1875–1949)

IN THE LATE NINETEENTH CENTURY and early twentieth century, proponents of oralism mounted a sustained and devastating campaign to "restore deaf people to society" through teaching deaf children to articulate and read lips and prohibiting them from signing. The oralism movement dovetailed perfectly with Social Darwinism, the prevailing philosophy of the times, through which the white, male, and, of course, hearing establishment persuaded itself that it was inherently superior. Schools for the Deaf laid off and ceased to hire Deaf teachers, including James Sowell, and oralism gained a near monopoly in the education of deaf children. Worse still for Deaf people, Alexander Graham Bell discouraged marriages between deaf people in order to prevent what he called a "deaf variety of the human race." However, America was large and democratic enough to allow dissent; the signing community held fast to its language and found ways to resist.

Many Deaf people thought oralists were more interested in the appearance of normalcy than in real education. In "The Oralist," Sowell goes so far as to call oralism a sin dealing in the sacrifice of souls. His quintessentially Deaf perspective runs through many of his poems, even his love poems, an area where most Deaf poets' work is indistinguishable from mainstream fare. James Nack may have waxed lyrical about his "blue-eye'd maid," but Sowell states a romantic as well as linguistic truth when he writes in "Dear Eyes of Grey" that his wife's eyes "speak a language."

James William Sowell became deaf in early infancy and attended the Alabama School for the Deaf. After graduating with the Gallaudet Class of 1900, he taught at the Maryland School for the Deaf while earning his master's degree in literature from Johns Hopkins University. Sowell married his Gallaudet sweetheart,

Maude Berizendine, and they settled in Omaha, where he began his teaching career in earnest at the Nebraska School for the Deaf. During the summers, he did doctoral work at the University of Nebraska, studying the development of literacy among Deaf students.

Sowell possessed "a peculiar ability" to teach his students the English language and a high appreciation of literature, something oralists thought only they could accomplish. He became principal of the school and editor of the school paper, and he wrote intensively in support of a sign-based method for educating Deaf children. His doctoral research was nearly complete when the state appointed a new superintendent for the school, who was a staunch oralist, and Sowell was relieved of his position as principal and later fired as a teacher. Because he had a growing family with roots already set deep in the Omaha signing community, he decided not to seek a new teaching job at another school. He instead worked as an accountant for Metropolitan Utilities District until his retirement. For many years, he had a column in the *Omaha World-Herald*, where he published most of his poetry.

James and Maude Sowell moved to Tucson, Arizona, to be near one of their daughters. Their son-in-law, Robert Morrow, was a teacher of the Deaf who became superintendent of the Arizona School for the Deaf and the Blind and, later, superintendent of the city school system. When Maude died in 1947, Sowell collected his poetry and published it privately as *To Her I Love*.

The Oralist*

All you care to do on earth is to make a show,
    Claim the power of miracle to see the people stare;
For you have an audience everywhere you go,
    Oralist, whose traffic is a little child's despair.

Oralist, O oralist, show your silken hose,
Little souls are sacrificed that you may wear such clothes;
Little souls and beautiful, pure from God's own hand;
    Halting feet that lamely walk; wistful eyes that plead,
Hearts but could you only read them, could you understand,
    You would throw away your creed and give to them their need.

Oralist, O oralist, work to get your laws
Force the baby lips to lisp, laugh at all their flaws.
Minds they have as sound as yours but for hours you waste;
    Spirits as impervious yearning for the light;
See! Their baby hands they lift, pleading that in haste
    You may see the wrong you do and will cease to smite.

Oralist, O oralist, turn your head aside,
Know you not the pitying Christ for sins like yours has died?

---

* Oralism is the educational method in which deaf children are taught speech and lipreading. "Pure" oralism prohibits any use of sign language.

Dear Eyes of Grey

Dear eyes of grey, I know not all you plead;
    Dear eyes, so full of meaning and of truth;
    Glad with affection's sweet and tender smile
    And beauty's tear which thrills with tremor sweet,
You speak a language, trusting eyes of grey.

Bright as a star that trembles 'neath the verge
    Of mimic storm clouds, closing o'er its light;
    Sad as the last lay of some pensive dove,
    Moaning its heart aches to the passing breeze,
As bright, as sad, dear trusting eyes of grey.

Ah, sad and sweet, as when in undertones
    Falls soul-felt music, tremulous and low;
    On dreamy ears when unto dreamy eyes
    Dear loved faces fading grow more faint
As sad, as sweet, dear trusting eyes of grey.

Dear as the first fond blush of early love,
    And fair as those that wrought when time was young
    A nation's fall; frank in their deepness, frank
    As a Madonna's raised to the sky,
O love's best gift, dear trusting eyes of grey.

Howard L. Terry
(1877–1964)

HOWARD L. TERRY's "On My Deafness" is only one of the many instances of Deaf poets rephrasing Keats's "melodies . . . unheard / Are sweeter" to explain how truth is found in silence. However, his long poem, "The Old Homestead," demonstrates that one does not experience the world in a lesser way because of deafness. It is richly textured, imbued with a striking sense of nostalgia for someone only nineteen years old, which Terry was when he reflected on the setting he found so comforting after the loss of his mother and after he recovered from a serious illness and experienced decreasing hearing. His boyhood days may have haunted him particularly due to his poor eyesight, in that people with limited vision absorb what they do see in a more heightened way than do people who have full use of vision. The poem must have been dear to him, for he held onto it for thirty-nine years before publishing it in his finest collection, *Sung in Silence: Selected Poems* (1929).

Howard L. Terry was born in St. Louis, Missouri, and experienced progressive deafness beginning in infancy. His mother died when he was eleven years old; he and his father then moved to Collinsville, Illinois. From a very young age, Terry wanted to be a writer, and he produced his first book at the age of fourteen. Although he attended public school and then a private academy, Terry described his education as "sadly neglected and misguided," especially in the English language. He did not learn sign language until he went to Gallaudet College in 1895. Because the college lacked accommodations for low-vision and blind students, however, he could not complete his studies.

In 1901, Terry married Alice Taylor, a Deaf woman he had known at Gallaudet, and they bought a farm in Missouri. Eight years later, they moved to California, where Alice blossomed as an activist in Deaf organizations. Terry wrote voluminously and published widely enough to be invited to become the editor of *Poetry World*, but he declined the offer, citing his eyesight. One of his novels, *A Voice from the Silence*, was successful enough to be optioned by a Hollywood film studio and to be reissued. He was responsible for the founding of the Guild of Deaf Writers, and he edited *Poems by the Deaf: An Anthology* (1942) with J. H. MacFarlane and Kate Shibley. In 1938, Gallaudet College awarded this "dean of deaf letters" an honorary degree.

From The Old Homestead

I. Retrospection

When time, as time has done and yet will do,
Outgrows the old to make way for the new,
The lonely heart, forgetting outward self,
And care and pain and riches, lowly pelf,
Allows itself to wander far away
To that sweet time when life was but a day
Of joy and sureness, love and sheer delight,
Untouched by wrong, e'er guided in the right
By loving hand of mother or of friend,
And dreams all this continues to life's end,
There comes some scene, some spot the best of all,
And this the memory does with joy recall.
Endearing moments, how ye hold and bind!
More than an idle musing of the mind,
For there is that within it, unexpressed,
That to the soul with sacredness is blessed,
And scenes by love engraved upon the heart
Remain a part of us until from life we part.

I hold most dear, with unexpressed love,
That scene, that home, where first I early strove,
And if these lines are efforts to reveal
My love of it, oh, break me every seal
That binds my heart, and from its depth let flow
Unchanged the current of my being's glow.

With that dark hour when I was an orphan made
A change came o'er that with me e'er has stayed:
A silent life, the slowly failing ear
In rural home I strive to picture here.
A humble house of unpretentious wood,
Wherein an aunt, long in her widowhood,

With daughters two engaged the lengthening years,
The business of life, the joys, the tears.
Such is the modest subject of my lines,
The spot for which my absent presence pines.
The house beside a mighty poplar stands,
Just where the roadway slopes to lower lands.
The weather-boarded sides its age extends,
And with that age a pleasing quaintness blends.
The overhanging roof and windows small
Full many a tale from out the past recall;
And there the swallow, nesting in the eaves,
Seeking their food a little family leaves,
High and secure beneath the sheltering board
The peeping fledglings wait the mother bird.
Their time to leave, like mine, was yet to come.
Might they, like me, recall their little home!
Within, the rooms are large and ceilings low,
Just as they made them many years ago;
And there the chimneys, piercing roof and floors.
The papered walls, the ever-creaking doors.
The narrow stair that to the garret lead,
For human comfort great improvement needs,
And youth must follow age to reach their height.
Such steps were never made for hurried flight.
The leaky roof, the rattling shutters green,
The cracking plaster and the cheesecloth screen;
The dear old garret of my boyhood day!
Bitter the winter chill and fierce the summer ray!

The goodly aunt who has the mother been
Through all my sickness and the trials within,
Has striven, and is striving while I write,
A child obedient to her God, a light
That through the sorrows she has had to bear
(And she had more than is just her share)
Has burned with one increasing radiance,
That will not flicker when the Maker's glance

Falls on it, as it will. Of her I speak,
But words are wanting and my lines are weak
And pay but poorly as a recompense
For all that she has done for me and my defense.
And I have seen her, tearful, in her pain,
When all our efforts to appease were vain;
When anguish, trouble, care and mental strife
Seemed on the verge of blotting out her life;
But then and there her Christian spirit told,
When rose she up to take another hold.
How many an act of kindliness has she
Put forth her efforts to extend to me!
And e'en the life that courses in these veins
I owe to her, to her and all her pains;
For once my pulse was slowly ebbing, when
With love and care she nursed me back again.
Should I not then outpour a thankful heart,
And in these lines my gratitude impart?
The daughters fair were kind and loving, too,
The one a teacher, in her letters true,
The other for the family played the cook,
And good she was at that, nor used a book
Of old recipes, with all its measures wrong.
Experience was her book, and well she got along.
The shelves of books the teacher's evening care,
The sister's thoughts were on our daily fare,
The mother dear and aunt her needle plied,
Managed the home and proved a loving guide.
Such was the little family of the place,
As best my pen in portraiture can trace.
A deep religious faith abided there,
Yet not so deep as ever to declare
Against the joys we were entitled to,
That drive our cares and spring the laughter true.
Religion is mysterious. Indeed,
When first we grasp it deeply must we plead
Within us, but the soul once on its track,

Increases strength no evil day can rack.
'Twas there I learned the Word, the godliness of grace,
Enough alone to bind me to the place.

Full every season had its days of joy,
And what a place to captivate a boy!
The spring, the summer, and the winter bare,
Youth found the thrill of pleasure everywhere!
Oh, might I have again one glorious hour;
I'd drain one cup and never ask for more.
The orchards lush, Pomona's smiling care,
Of autumn nutting Nature gave our share;
The fishing streams, the lakes, the shady lanes,
The fields of grain that swelled with summer rains,
The harvest days, the harvest moon, the night
That softly mellowed all the picture bright.
On glassy pond in winter time we'd glide,
And hills there were on runner's edge to slide.
The marshy lakes—who sought the wary duck
Could get him had he half a hunter's luck.
And he who sought the solitary wood
To roam therein in meditative mood,
Need but to follow yonder streamlet's flow,
And be alone where reeds and violets blow.
There was a shadowed spot beside the stream
Where I was wont to sit alone and dream.
And thereabouts might poets love to roam,
Forget the world, and make a poet's home;
Where Solitude and Goodness dwelt as one,
And foliaged treetops hid the summer sun.
Enchanted spot that soothed my yearning soul,
Still may ye be, howe'er the seasons roll!
Oh, happy place! Should not a youthful heart
Rejoice in what such places rare impart?
How transitory, though, these wholesome joys.
We have them for a time, when Time destroys
The spirit and the zeal that filled us then,

Nor condescends to give them back again.
A melancholy thought it were, indeed,
Did Providence not kindly intercede,
And while Time steals from us a goodly thing,
Yet ever in our pathway does he bring,
Appropriate to our years, a newer way
To pass our days, though not so flush and gay.

On My Deafness

All things go well until they feel His wrath.
O silence, there are marvels in thy state!
Flora may bud and bloom despite the drouth,
Impelled of God, and I, despite my fate,
Believing, yet may bloom in fairer fields.
If listening inwardly to unheard sound
Is reaping all that's best, what silence yields,
Then sound deceives; truth is in silence found.

Alice Jane McVan
(1906–1970)

DEAF PEOPLE HAVE OFTEN identified themselves with other oppressed people and their histories and struggles. This is why Alice Jane McVan can write with personal authority in "And No Applause" about the pressures of bowing to the white man's laws. The white man is, of course, also hearing, and the tightrope act McVan writes of is evocative of Deaf people's straining to speak properly and decipher speech visually, which McVan herself did, to perform the thankless task of acting hearing. Yet it is not quite applause that she is seeking. In "Response," McVan rejects pity and, instead, demands the right to fend for herself and to be angry, "for anger is the swift response of equals."

Alice Jane McVan was born in Pittsburgh, Pennsylvania. When she was eight, her family moved to Buffalo, New York, where she attended public school until she became deaf, and then she transferred to St. Mary's School for the Deaf. McVan graduated after two years and entered Gallaudet College, where she became the first female editor of *The Buff and Blue* (the college newspaper). She received her degree in 1928 and obtained a job as a teacher at St. Mary's School for the Deaf. She stayed there for two years before accepting a job in the publications department of the Hispanic Society of America in New York City.

In 1938, McVan married Karl Bernard Stein, but the marriage failed and she remained single thereafter. During World War II, she taught English and citizenship to deaf refugees from Europe under the New York Division of Vocational Rehabilitation. Throughout her career at the Hispanic Society, McVan did extensive research in Spanish culture and published many articles and translations, including a definitive text on the life and work of Spanish poet Antonio Machado. In 1953, the Hispanic Society of America published her collection of poetry, *Tryst*. In 1959, during one of her trips to Spain, the Spanish signing community honored her with a ball featuring translations of her poetry in Spanish Sign Language and dance.

McVan retired in 1966, due to ill health, and moved to St. Louis to spend time with her sister. At the time of her death, she was living in a nursing home.

And No Applause

They live
balanced
on a tight rope
of fear,
aloof
from the warmth
and safety
down here;
like acrobats,
dreading
a move timed wrong,
an interval held
a second too long,
alert,
aware
that everywhere
security fades
in shifting air,
transient, frail—
tomorrow? now?—
response may falter,
judgment fail;
they taste the fear
before the fact,
before the turn,
the innocent act
that lurches to
the sudden slip,
the just-missed grip;
tense,
they hear
with quiet face
the white man's sneer,

and bow
with grace
to white men's laws.
Only this:
there are
no spangled tights,
no rolls of drums,
no colored lights,
no net,
and no applause.

Response

With the hardness and the purity of anger turns upon me!
Let the heat of white-hot anger sear my brain,
let the claws of fury rake my heart and body,
for I promise you I shall forget the pain,
the wounds so made and cauterized at once
will quickly heal, the scars as quickly fade,
and I shall then have ratified the contract
that Life and I together duly made.

But spare me the indignity, the dishonor of your pity!
Let no morsel of the soft, corroding stuff
be pressed upon me with your pseudo-kindness;
I must endure, grow valiant and tough.
Let me expiate my anger on you, also,
let me coil the flame of wrath about your soul,
for anger is the swift response of equals
and pity is the victor's loathsome dole.

Earl Sollenberger
(c. 1912–1947)

EARL SOLLENBERGER'S SENSITIVITY to any attempts by others to control him comes not only from him being a Deaf person but also a Jewish-American man. With a chip on each shoulder, he wrote poetry that is ahead of his time in that it exhibits the spirit of the Deaf Pride movement, which did not begin until three decades after his death. "The Legend of Simon Simplefuss" is a satirical self-portrait of an "ancient freak" told in the third person, while "Thoughts in a Pennsylvania Cornfield" probes deeper into how Sollenberger felt at odds with society and its insistence on defining what is "normal." His "Reply to 'Beware Lest People Think—'" is indeed a refusal to fit in a mold.

What may be more striking than the dissent in his work is Sollenberger's voice. Self-deprecating, ironic, and threaded with sly humor, it closely resembles the tone of Jewish-American literature of his generation and what would emerge in Deaf literature after his death. But he wrote one poem devoid of his customary irony—"To a Neglected Poet," which he dedicated to Howard L. Terry.

The two poets could not be more different. Terry wrote very little on deafness, while Sollenberger was only too happy to stir up controversy by using his deafness as a strong spice in the mix. Terry was a traditionalist whereas Sollenberger was an avant-garde who regularly visited Greenwich Village. Yet Sollenberger is sincere in saluting his elder fellow Deaf poet, a testament to the powerful link in their shared identity. Unlike the general poetry community, the community of Deaf poets is far too small for any clashing literary schools to usurp the tolerance and affection Deaf poets have for one another.

Earl Sollenberger, a native of Chambersburg, Pennsylvania, became deaf at age six when a horse kicked his head. He attended

Gallaudet College, where he wrestled and wrote essays, stories, and poetry for the school paper, *The Buff and Blue*. "Solly" graduated from Gallaudet College with the Class of 1934. This statistician's collections of poetry are *Along With Me* (1937) and *Handful of Quietness* (1941), both published with artwork by fellow Deaf poet Felix Kowalewski. The well-liked but moody poet killed himself with a butcher knife to his throat in 1947.

The Legend of Simon Simplefuss
(Without Benefit of Sound)

> I hope it is no crime
> To laugh at all things. For I wish to know
> What, after all, are all things—but a show?
> —Lord Byron

Better by far this wretch were dead
Who rashly from his people fled;
What does his freedom now avail?
He merely moved to deeper Hell.
He thought he would ambition try,
But soon he finds desires too high
Will bring his beanstalk down with cramps.

All jest aside, how far he stamps
And wide, falls short of being long—
Falls short, I mean, of righting wrong.
On every hand he is denied,
And it is he for whom Christ cried;
But cries of Christ be far away,
And preachers use their time to pray.
He goes alone, and church and state
Cannot be bothered by his fate,
Just so he keeps right side of them.

One person knows he is a gem
The dark, unfathomed bums surmount,
But that's himself, and does not count.
He may make friends, but cannot hold
A fille de joie, except by gold.
Past dancing halls he wends his way;
The whispering wind fears he will stay,
But being wise, he pushes on
The way his fellow Cains have gone.

He dare not join the corner group
For they will make of him a dupe.
The radio and talkie reel
Are quite above this man's appeal.

A dog may let him scratch its neck
Until he speaks! his voice's wreck
Would even to a cat convey
The sense to keep out of his way.
His joys are limited to books
And marigolds and babless brooks;
Or he may share his company
In silent séance with the sea.
He even may eke out some fun
In gazing at the clouds and sun;
But no man of the normal race
Can jest with this guy face to face.

If wandering from the neighborhood,
He seeks the solace of the wood,
No ravished virgin's cries he'll heed,
But if he senses madam's need
And sends the tactless villain flying,
Her frenzied words will want replying,
At which she'll think her life at stake
And yell for succor to the rake.

He cannot win; that fact is settled,
And reader, if you're somewhat nettled
As to the nature of this being,
Let me explain, that you on seeing
This Terror, won't be put to fleeing.
He's neither Eskimo nor Zulu,
Nor gorilla—I wouldn't fool you.

This creature is an ancient freak—
He's deaf, and disinclined to speak!

Birds Will Sing

Heard melodies are sweet, but those unheard
Are sweeter.
—John Keats

> To a thrush on a mulberry bough,
> Once on a time God said:
> "Sing, little fellow, sing
> A sweet tune for that girl there
> On the lawn.
> She is watching, she is waiting,
> She is listening, listening, listening."
>
> The bird sang.
>
> At the end God said:
>
> "That was a good song. My choir
> Back home was listening in,
> And I think that We
> Shall have better music from now on.
> That girl there
> Couldn't hear you,
> But she is satisfied too."

Reply to "Beware Lest People Think—"

I thank you for your warning, dear, but I
Can't cater to what people think or say
In this one case! Like gentle you I try
From fear, perhaps, to let them have their way
In customs, methods, points of view, and laws—
In everything I guess; except this case!
And it is vain obeisance, vain because
In spite of all I do to hold a place
Of "self-respect" the damners know me well,
And I am damned for this if not for that
Till there is little left to think or tell.
So in my verse I put my thoughts in flat
Non-paying words; if sex, then SEX: it's "art."
Be damned or not I'll pen what's in my heart.

Thoughts in a Pennsylvania Cornfield

John can cut faster than I can; he always
Is way ahead. He makes the "bucks" and ties the stalks together
Shock after shock. No wonder! That comes of college.
That comes of fooling away at thoughts and theories
Which tend to make one moody and slow. If knowing
Were happiness, I still would have cause to be wretched,
Dreading the hour when the worms that filled my body,
Busy, would not ask the questions that might save me.
What is the upshot of it all then? Little.
My brain will not taste better for being wiser.
To men: so to worms; but I have a feeling
The worms will know whether or not I was potent—
As does a dog that curiously sniffs me over,
And counts the women I have lain with, judging
Me accordingly. The brain heads the host of pretenders:
What is intellect? What money? The only power
Respected by earth and dumb things is virility.
Those born to live simply have no need of quibbling;
They come at once to the purpose of their being.

Take John there. What makes him so tireless?
You will say that this is his land, his duty,
That he promised someone so much corn by October,
And that he is a regular hellhound for money.
All that may be true, but listen, it is truer
That behind your reasoning, behind John's reasons
Surges the dominating will of the sperm cells.
Let his mind tell him lies; the worms will know better
He works for his loving—his wife and his children.
Now hear that dog; he is always barking or howling,
Complaining against everything and everybody.
I think he should be mated or buried;
The devil, if not we, may grant him room to live in.

I am getting pretty sacrilegious lately;
That comes of perusing weighty books and dreaming.
I wish now that I had never gone to college;
I would much rather be like John and mind my chopping
Than dwell upon thoughts that men have been hanged for expressing.

These weeds are awful: "Stinking Toms," ground cherries,
Burdocks and thistles, artichokes, morning glories,
And the worst are the entangling morning glories.
At school I had always defended morning glories,
Calling them flowers, not weeds. Don't ask if I am sorry;
We are a week behind now with corn not worth cutting.
How often the thing we treasure and call our dearest
Sooner or later gets in our way! Oh the pity
Of a purgatory between a loss and a surfeit.
I will not then, find fault with the morning glories.
John said he had planted corn here a bit too often;
Now the place is swarming with weeds! Look yonder
Where the cow is grazing; you don't see a weed there.
John calls it "virgin soil," and he says, next season,
He will plant his corn there; then there will be no reason
To denounce such beautiful things as morning glories.
Too often people floating upon the surface
Of water and stuff that is life, forget that below them,
Rather than with them, lies the force that supports them.
If they knew this, there would not be so much of blaming,
So much of complaining, protesting, and sorrow.
For then they could easily solve the problem,
To put the solution simply, by moving the cornfield.
That would spare them their disillusion of beauty.

Oh well, we are nearly through now . . . I guess most people
Think the same way about life: "We're nearly through now."
If they can't harrow a fertile cornfield, see them
Cleave to a poor one, and somehow struggle through it.
Why don't they rise and demand rich cornfields or nihil?

That I can tell you. You see the cornstalk tassels?
You see the silk on each ear of corn. Nature
Is a sly goddess, ruling with only one weapon,
And she uses it well, holding it suspended
Over our hearts like the heavy sword of the master
That once threatened Damocles, and Nature in triumph
Takes herself off and leaves us writing in anguish,
But forced to live—with a sword over our cornfields;
With the shadow of the sword on our cornfields.

Ah futility! Here I am back again where I started,
Thinking thoughts men have been hanged for expressing.
I knew that my mind would not be misled by quibbling,
But would soon compel me to get down to business.
My psychology professor once said that quibbling
Was useful. Of course he didn't say "quibbling."
I think he called it "rationalization,"
And laughing, he said he couldn't live without it.
I knew what he meant, but after a lot of thinking:
In this world there are less truths worth saying
Than I have fingers, and they are so easy,
By taking notes of our needs, to discover.
The thing that really counts is how to express them;
If you don't express them right, it's a hanging matter.
It is all right for a cornstalk to grow unblushing,
Or a dog to live, or want to live (oh that howling!)
Unashamed. But with people it's another matter.

The sun is now setting behind the mountains.
It is leaving our cornfields in concealing darkness
That we may not wither in the sunshine, working
On principles of rationalization as John is;
But that we may directly make mightier the silken
Thread trembling under the weight of the threatening
Sword of Damocles. In New York bankers and beachcombers
Are doing it now for their cornfields, for their country,

But mostly for themselves, for their thirst, unable
To do otherwise. Last summer at Coney Island
I met a beachcomber at work in the early morning,
Sifting sand by the side of the singing Atlantic,
And I inquired of him what he had to live for.
"Gin and a woman, what else?" was his answer.
I have heard that before, but never from a banker
Or a college professor, but like the beachcomber
They are now undoubtedly in the arms of their women,
Unblushing and unashamed, blessing the darkness
Not with words, but with the frenzy of their breathing;
Mouth to mouth, thigh to thigh, past all thought of quibbling,
In sacred séance, anointed with their own moisture,
Silent, holy, anointed with work-sweat of their bodies,
With one will like a river of molten metal:
Fierce with the increasing charge of electricity,
Bright with a brilliance that scars and dazzles,
Rushing towards the brink of a mystic Niagara,
So to end the merciless, magnetizing current;
With agonized impatience to be hurdled
To the very vortex of the generator,
Bearing the precious accumulated burden,
Trembling in every fibre with fierceness,
Fearing lest they faint and defeat their purpose,
For they have endured much for the sake of fulfillment,
For the sake of peaceful ease of slumber—
To sleep on the sweetness of travail shortly over.

This is why strong men often woo the weakness of dying,
Why wealthy women seek death from arsenic vials;
The pain of their loving outweighs their joy of living.
Poets do not stoop to quibble in this matter.
This accounts in full for so many saddened poets.
Neither can the women escape, but the women know it—
The colonel's lady and sister Judy O'Grady,
The Sapphos, Juliets, Heloises, and Greek Helens,

Not forgetting Vanessa—what did Swift say about her
And himself?—Something like this, as I remember:

> "What success sweet Vanessa met
> Is to the world a secret yet.
> Whether the nymph, to please her swain,
> Talks in a high, romantick strain,
> Or whether he at least descends
> To act with less seraphick ends;
> Or to compound the business, whether
> They temper love and books together,
> Must never to mankind be told,
> Nor shall the conscious muse unfold."

That is the difference in morals the world over.
Some people just keep their faces cleaner than others.
But when loving Vanessa found that Swift was married,
She died heartbroken. There is a woman for you!
John says to quit. I guess it is time I quit thinking
Thoughts like these that men have been hanged for expressing.
It is too dangerous to be different. Maybe some girl
Will take in a movie with me tonight, then
Maybe some dancing, supper, or something after.

To a Neglected Poet

A poet is a thing that starves to death.
—Howard L. Terry

> Terry, old soldier, let me try to write
> A sonnet's worth of thanks for what you sent—
> Your sparkling poems! You are here tonight,
> Speaking to me, brilliant and eloquent.
>
> Reading, I hear you—while I realize
> The poet's fate your life too clearly shows:
> Beauty the lure, and bitterness the prize,
> While life limps slowly to its tragic close.
>
> "First of all and sweetest singer born,"
> Terry, my anger rises and subsides,
> Shifting from humor to despair, that scorn
> As you received, your chief reward provides . . .
>
> But I have heard you sing, and to my soul
> Your soul appeared, defiant, buoyant, whole.

Felix Kowalewski
(1913–1989)

Aside from penning the obligatory tributes to his teachers and to leaders of the signing community of his time, Felix Kowalewski's poetry is surprisingly negative and, at times, despairing. This is surprising because he graduated from a residential school for the Deaf and then from Gallaudet, where he had access to the positive cultural perspective of deafness. Perhaps the despondency in his work can be explained by the combination of factors exemplified by his three poems included here, which correspond with his experiences.

Although Kowalewski met with rapid success as an artist when he was a young man—winning international recognition, no less—he struggled to continue in that trajectory and became bitter, disappointed, and, according to his students, angry. His long-time friend Eric Malzkuhn believed that "I Will Take My Dreams . . . " was written during a time when Kowalewski seriously contemplated suicide. This brings up the possibility that he was depressed. However, his fixation on deafness as the cause of his sorrow and despair may have masked the true cause of his depression.

In "Heart of Silence," despite the use of the most beautiful visual description—literally painting with words—Kowalewski feels forsaken, as if what beauty he sees only reminds him of what he thinks he is missing. He also identifies himself with Victor Hugo's deaf hunchback of Notre Dame in "Quasimodo May Not Dare." Like the hunchback, the narrator of this poem is rejected by a woman. No doubt Kowalewksi was alert to any form of discrimination, but this very personal rejection may have served to reinforce his negative feelings about his deafness. If audism acts in the same way racism does, then what W. E. B. Du Bois and James

Baldwin say applies: The real danger lies not in the white man hating the black man but in the black man hating himself.

Felix Kowalewski was born to Polish immigrants in Brooklyn, New York. Deafened at six by spinal meningitis, he attended the New York School for the Deaf at Fanwood. There, he began his long and distinguished career as an artist, winning a national soap sculpture contest and studying at the New York School of Fine and Applied Art during his senior year. At Gallaudet College, President Percival Hall recognized Kowalewski's talents and arranged for him to study watercoloring under David Kline. Before graduating from Gallaudet in 1937, he had already exhibited his artwork at numerous venues, including the International Exhibition of Fine and Applied Art by Deaf Artists of 1934.

Between 1937 and 1955, Kowalewksi taught art at the West Virginia School for the Deaf, the Michigan School for the Deaf, and the California School for the Deaf at Berkeley before settling at the California School for the Deaf at Riverside (CSDR) until his retirement in 1977. In addition to his teaching, he worked in a wide variety of media, exhibited coast to coast, and published art criticism, biographies of other Deaf artists, and his own poetry. His collection of poems, *You and I*, is a classic example of a strictly Deaf publication venture. It was produced in 1983 by the printing department of CSDR, without distributorship but advertised and sold primarily to Deaf readers.

I Will Take My Dreams . . .

I will take my dreams to the top of the highest mountain.
I will take my dreams, I will take them all.
I will wrap them up in a cloak of silver.
I will roll them to the top, like a snowy ball.
I will take my dreams to the top of the highest mountain,
And then I will stop and rest a while;
I will open my cloak and spread them out before me—
I will talk to them, I will dip my hands in the shimmering pile.

Oh, here is a dream of a beautiful lady, gracious and golden;
And here is a dream that is bitterly sweet.
Here is a dream, that has never been ended;
And here is a dream of forever dancing feet.

Here is a dream of dragons and witches and goblins,
And here is a dream of fairies and djinns;
And here sings a dream of a beautiful music
—A music of hautboys and violins.

I will dream my dreams on the top of the highest mountain.
I will kiss their hands, I will cry "farewell."
I will bind them up once more in my cloak of silver—
Each little hand, each silverly pealing bell.

I will stand with my dreams on the top of the highest mountain;
I will brush from my hands the dust of their tears.
I will stride to the edge of the abyss before me—
The yawning abyss of dreamless years.

I will seize my dreams on the top of the highest mountain;
And then, in despair, I will fling them down!
I will see them fall, to burst in a thousand fragments
—The fairies, the music, the lovely lady's crown!

Felix Kowalewski   117

I will sit me down on the top of the highest mountain.
I will stare at the lonely waste of rock and sky.
I will lay me down at the edge of the abyss.
I will dream no more; and dreamless, I shall die.

Heart of Silence

Hastening clouds and the sudden sunlight after
A caressing shower of April rain.
I stand beneath the elm tree
And watch the pale green buds rustle and glisten;
My hair is wet and my clothes asteam
With musky vapors—my hands I thrust
Into my pockets, for a sudden chill
Runs down my spine. A scurrying cloud
Obscures the sun for a moment—the edges are silver.
It passes on and the radiant orb
Bursts forth once more in an exultant splendor
Of sheer white light. I close my eyes . . .
"Beauty!" I cry, and I am answered
As a dew-drop falls upon my cheek,
Trembles, and then—in a joyous cascade
Runs down the ridge of my jawbone
And is lost in the cleft of my chin.

I stand alone beneath the glistening elm tree
And watch the red sun sinking in the west.
All around me I glimpse a subtle motion—
A hidden rustling in the dewy grass,
The friendly elm wavers beside me
And o'er my head the whispering branches hover
With their pale green shoots of murmuring leaves.
Lost in an endless quietude, my wandering gaze
Is caught by the sudden bursting
Of a pale green bud on a branch close by.
All of this motion and a rising breeze
Touch on my wavering heart that cries for sound.
Thus I have stood while countless Aprils
Have come and gone and with them rainy leas
Of velvety green, and palpitating motion . . .

And always I have listened with empty ears
To all this beauty and stilled the hidden pain
That surged throughout my silent heart.

I stand alone beneath the wavering elm tree
And watch the evening sky grow dim;
The grass and the tree beside me dance and waver
Like beautiful ghosts in the gathering darkness.
. . . Night falls and I do not hear it.
Silence envelopes me with a cloak profound,
A saffron moon glimmers through the dark void.
And still I stand, motionless, mute and expectant—
Waiting, waiting—as I have always waited—
For this silent heart to break. Again, in vain!
And again I cry to the silence "Forsaken!"
And stumble home through the darkness again.

Quasimodo May Not Dare

Lady, when first I looked into your eyes
Across the tennis-table, when I came
To this glad place, I sought to know your name—
But never spoke to you in any wise
For a long while, till the swift-moving hours
And constant meeting gave me grace to say
Simply "Good Morning." (Darling!) "Will you play?"
And daily you'd defeat me, sun or showers.
Beloved, if you knew how dear your smile
Has grown to me through all these days and nights,
Disgustedly you'd knock me from the heights
Of quiet love, with a few words: "That vile
Old deaf-mute! Now—whatever made him think . . . ?"
And into deeper silence I shall sink.

Loy E. Golladay
(1914–1999)

NOT ONLY WAS Loy E. Golladay the first poet to devote the bulk of his poetry to Deaf subjects, but much of his work is also sunny, celebratory, and humorous. In other words, he was a poet of the Deaf Pride movement. Earl Sollenberger, his close contemporary, died before the movement began rolling in earnest after 1960. Felix Kowalewski, another close friend, did not have the sensibility to embrace the movement. So it is Golladay's work that marks a significant turning point in Deaf American poetry.

Praising American Sign Language (ASL), paying homage to interpreters, poking fun at linguists teaching ASL to monkeys, and keeping the "Deaf Poets Society" tradition of writing in reply to other Deaf poets, Golladay's range was such that he served as a kind of poet laureate. Although they are not included here, he wrote some poems in "ASL style." And his funny anecdote-as-poem "Incident at the B.M.T." particularly shows him in lockstep with Deaf Pride literature, one of whose landmark and best-selling texts was Roy Holcomb's 1977 book of anecdotes in the same vein called *Hazards of Deafness*.

Loy E. Golladay was born in Virginia's Fort Valley and contracted spinal meningitis at eight. He began his writing career while a student at the Virginia School for the Deaf, winning a major mainstream magazine essay contest. He graduated from Gallaudet College in 1934, along with fellow Deaf poet Earl Sollenberger. Golladay married his college sweetheart. He earned postgraduate degrees from Gallaudet (1942) and the University of Hartford (1958).

His distinguished teaching career, which spanned forty-five years, began at the West Virginia School for the Deaf. When he transferred to the American School for the Deaf (ASD), Golladay renewed the community's interest in the school's history and its cofounder, Laurent Clerc. The school's museum was later named in Golladay's honor. In 1969, Golladay joined Robert F. Panara at the National Technical Institute for the Deaf, where he became its first Professor Emeritus in 1980. His poetry was collected and published by ASD in 1991 as *A Is for Alice*.

On Seeing a Poem Recited in Sign Language

We watched the far-off vision in your eyes,
Your lovely hands make paraphrase in air
Of shape and shade no artist can surprise
In paint or sculpture, nor the ballet's rare
And lively grace. Your fluent gestures share
The freedom of the wind, the crash of ocean,
The arcs that Euclid traced; but yet more fair,
The onomatopoetics of motion . . .
And while your vibrant silence glows and glooms,
The harpsichord, the violin are mute.
You finish, bow. Applause resounds the room,
And voices rise. I pause, irresolute:
Was it of Israel alone in whom
It once was said, his heart-strings are a lute?

Silent Homage

(For an Interpreter)

The moving lips speak voicelessly—but hark:
The winged words fly from your fluttering hands;
And each who dwells in silence, understands
How dawn, the rosy-fingered, burns the dark
From shadow worlds wherein the teeming brain
Lay, like a captive, in a dungeon cell;
Your magic bursts the iron citadel,
And breaks the lock, and brings the light again.
Dear friend, how empty, vain and commonplace
Must seem this gratitude we bring to you;
Yet now we render homage, as your due,
Remembering your patience, love and grace—
With twining fingers as you blithely go,
Daily, to fell our Walls of Jericho.

Footnote to Anthropological Linguistics I
(Washoe No. 1)*

When Ph.D.s taught Washoe how to sign
And all her cousins—somewhere down the line
Some chimpanzee (they said) will be so smart
He'll be the human genius counterpart.
He's sure to get here sometime, soon or late—
So teach these monkeys to communicate!

And, sure enough, there came upon the scene
A monkey savant with a face serene,
Bespectacled, benign. He went to Yale,
Plus M.I.T. and Stanford (each detail
Of all their knowledge fed into his brain
By interpreters—let me here explain).

At length this ape consented to digress
From all his scholarship to meet the press.
They crowded in with TV, pad and pen,
From Gotham, Paris, Rome, and West Cheyenne,
The newshawks tense, the newshens pert and pearled,
All set to scoop a wan and waiting world.

With Reasoner and Walters in the van,
He spoke in S.E.E. and Ameslan:†
"In search of selfish prestige, power and pelf,
The man has made a monkey of himself.
This theory of Darwin's is the bunk,
For clearly Man is father to the monk!"

---

* Washoe, a chimpanzee captured in the wild in 1966, was the subject of anthropologists Allen and Beatrice Gardner's study to demonstrate that another species could acquire human language.

† S.E.E. refers to Signing Exact English, an artificial communication system that uses modified ASL signs in English word order. Ameslan was a popular abbreviation for American Sign Language.

Footnote to Anthropological Linguistics II
(Washoe No. 2)

When Washoe's grandson also learned to sign,
(Chimpanzee genius of the family line)
At interpreting he could not be beat;
He signed with equal skill—both hands and feet.
    It was a marvel of bilingual grace.
    He added footnotes at the proper place.

With wages a banana split or two,
He'd translate all day long the ballyhoo
At big conventions (using signs bi-level).
At R.I.D. the prexy raised the devil*
    "That's monkey business," swore he to his neighbor.
    "We're ruined by this cheap chimpanzee labor!"

The N.A.D. got the I.R.S. okay
For tax deductions on the day-to-day
Expense of keeping, for each deaf householder,
A private interpreter on his shoulder.
    (By then they'd developed by careful breeding
    A compact model, needing little feeding.)

It was a charming sight to see some cute
And cuddly interpreters dressed in suits
To ape their owners, chattering away,
Both hand and foot, to pass the time of day;
    When, I suspect, some naughty ape offender
    Might sometimes tell a tale of double entendre.

Those apes learned fast, though learning out of school;
They unionized to shed their owners' rule.

---

* R.I.D. is the Registry of Interpreters for the Deaf, the leading organization and certification program for interpreters in the United States; "prexy" means president.

To cap these 'monkey-signs,' their revolution
Took over R.I.D.'s old constitution,
  And voted in, effective that November,
  Each human "terp" an honorary member!

But ape ambition moved them to excel.
All these sign systems! Why not 'M.S.L.'?
(Which no one understands—I guarantee,
Unless a real, card-carrying chimpanzee!)
  And so, at last, the human 'terps' prevail.
  No moral here. So ends this monkey tale.

Surely the Phoenix

(In reply to a poem by Felix Kowalewski)

You who have hurled your dreams from the highest mountain;
You who have lain down dreamless to die—
Ruthlessly torn away their clinging fingers,
Banished their faces and turned to a dreamless sky:

All of you fancies, your bright dream children—
O, can you remember how they laughed and played;
Light wit on their lips, heart brimming with music,
The lovely, laughing ladies—have they been dismayed?

The lands afar that beckoned, the temple bells turned silver—
Have the bells been strangely silenced, lands sunk beneath the sea,
Their splendid cities shattered and the ruined ramparts haunted
By a dreamer's dream that dwindles constantly?

You who have hurled your dreams from the highest mountain,
And watched their splintering crash to the ground;
Did you see all the stars that were torn from their courses?
Surely the universe shook at the sound!

And the wind-worn stones on a burning wasteland
Gave tone to a voiceless, desolate cry,
And a mountain cracked and a charnel city
Thrust its bones to a blood-red sky.

Surely the dreams go on forever,
Surely the phoenix arises again!
The seed, though purged in the searing ashes,
Will raise its face to the singing rain.

Nothing begins where nothing ended,
All things enter whence all things fly;
Surely the dreams go on forever—
Only the dreamers die.

Die, then they cast away their dreaming,
When they scorn the grain in the search for chaff.
Then Death sits back in his gloomy cavern
To laugh . . . and laugh . . . and laugh.

Incident at the B.M.T.

There at the subway entrance,
shooting the breeze
with eloquent hands and fingers.
Being deaf
(not necessarily dumb)—
Merely—
"not inclined to speak,"
we three friends were accosted
by this lady.

Lips mumbling,
gabble-gabble-gabble—
obviously asking
Where . . . how . . . which way?

We couldn't hear
the sound of her voice—
obviously, because
(for one thing)
we weren't listening.

My friend Felix,
He's got technique:
He gestured and pointed:

Down, right, left,
right again.
There you are.

She smiled thanks,
and bustled off.

Three minutes later,
she flounced back,
mad as a hornet;
approached Felix,
bent her umbrella
over his head;
then marched back
in a huff.

Curious,
we went to investigate:
Down, right, left,
right again.
There it was:

MEN'S ROOM.

Rex Lowman
(1918–2001)

TREATING DEAFNESS AS A source of alienation, being strange and even not of the earth, Rex Lowman's poetry has a strong taste for deliberate metaphors and a brooding language. In "Bitterweed," bitterness is a foreigner's tool for survival as a foreigner, where the only means for securing respect is through answering hate with hate. "Beethoven" has history's most famous deaf man, a "cold angel hurled / From sound to silence," a wounded creature working on a kind of revenge, not unlike the bitterweed in the first poem here. While the third poem obliquely praises the majesty of signing, Lowman imbues it with ambiguous, otherworldly qualities that serve to set it apart from ordinary life down on earth to the signing community.

Whatever feelings Lowman harbored about his deafness early in his creative work, his poems became mellow in later years. But he retained some bitterness, according to his one-time student and Deaf poet Raymond Luczak, bitterness not against deafness but against poetry. He was apparently disappointed in his career as a poet and advised Luczak against pursuing a vocation in the art both of them so clearly excelled in.

Rex Lowman was born in Prattsville, Arkansas. He became deaf at three following a tonsillectomy. After graduating from the Arkansas School for the Deaf in 1936, Lowman made a name for himself at Gallaudet College by winning three straight first prizes in an intercollegiate poetry competition sponsored by the American Association of University Women. He graduated from Gallaudet in 1940 and earned his master's degree in economics from American University. Lowman married in 1943 and had two children.

He taught at the Georgia and Virginia Schools for the Deaf and worked for the U.S. Census Bureau; the Department of Health, Education, and Welfare; and the Brookings Institution before beginning his long career at Gallaudet in 1954. Lowman retired as chair of the economics department in 1989. He published in 1964 a collection of poems, *Bitterweed*, and until his death, continued to publish his poetry, especially in Deaf publications.

Bitterweed

Beware the dark eyes on you in the street
And the impersonal glances
Of those who pass you by—
They have no love for you, though you be their brother;
Though you should cry for pity, there would be none.

Growing in alien soil, the strange plant dies
From rocks that press too hard, that block its root,
Sent underground for nourishment in earth
That holds no sustenance for such as come
Unbidden through the tunnel of the rain.
Wherever you may go, the word shall pass
That you are stranger there, and you shall know
That unreceptive ground and fierce sunlight
In the press of hostile faces: they will shout
In a bitter voice the wisdom of the old,
Who have no will to live nor strength to die
And speak the blind prejudice of the stone,
And close the shadowy door.

Only the bitterweed can sink its root
Into the powerful rancor of the soil
And blossom forth in strong integrity,
Undaunted by a hatred. You must send
Your anger forth to rend the strangling rock
And with your strength build shelter from the sun;
And send them also
A word as bitter as theirs, as filled with hatred:
Then only will they let you pass in peace.

Beethoven

This tree is music; and this rose
Is laughter rippling on a stream
Free-flowing into hills of dream
Grown phantasmal in evening's close.
The counterpoint of wind that blows
In faint, elusive gusts is theme
For all the undertones that teem
In glimmering light which fades and glows.
This woodland that is yet a world,
Peopled with all that Eden held,
Has one cold angel, forthwith hurled
From sound to silence,—he who felled
The ululation of this wound
With all the instruments of sound.

Wingéd Words

Only the wind can bring your voice tonight
And only wind can speak the subdued thunder
That is the speech of wingéd men flying under
High cirrus clouds, drenched in a haze of light.
Only the shadow of your passing flight
Against the moon can rend our hearts asunder
From their new fear and stir again to wonder
The riven mind that knew an empty height.
For you are not of this earth from whom there passes
This curious, this indistinctive speech
That holds the rustling of terrestrial grasses
And sound of silence in the very breach
Of space profound. Even a godhead girds
Its majesty upon these wingéd words.

Robert F. Panara
(1920–)

"ON HIS DEAFNESS," Robert F. Panara's poem about tinnitus and how reading makes him feel as if he can hear, is the most widely anthologized and quoted poem by a Deaf writer. It serves both hearing people who wonder what Deaf people "hear" and Deaf people who wish to find an expression for what they experience, for whom the word "silence" is never accurate. Panara wrote many poems that are useful in this way, and "Lip Service" and "Ars Poetica" are such poems: one reminds us that talk of communication means nothing to the Deaf until signing comes into the equation, and the other offers advice to aspiring Deaf poets that, the joking aside, is genuinely helpful. "Idylls of the Green" is not only a fine example of many poems written by Gallaudet alumni about their college days—which continue to be profoundly memorable, as more and more students have their first encounter with Deaf culture there—but is also interesting in that it closely resembles much of Panara's prose writing. It is abundantly peppered with idioms that come with quotation marks, reflecting the peculiar habit of many Deaf people who graduated high school before 1980 of signing quotation marks before employing an English idiom by fingerspelling or transliteration.

For a long period in the history of the education of Deaf children, it was not enough for students to acquire a good command of the English language; they also needed to have an *idiomatic* command of it. Although Panara did not grow up at a Deaf school, he must have picked up on the quoting of idioms as a status symbol for the level of one's education. It served to impress other Deaf people more than it did hearing people, for hearing people do not use so many idioms so close to one another; instead, they pass them off nonchalantly, without thinking of it. The campaign to teach Deaf children how to use idioms—spanning from the publication of James Lewis Smith's lexicons in 1905 and 1912 to the community-wide bestseller *A Dictionary of Idioms for the Deaf*, published by the American School for the Deaf in 1966—had the result of many Deaf people being more hearing than the hearing in their writing. Nevertheless, this did lend a special flavor to the language of writers who used it well, and it certainly was a good tool for Panara's art and teaching.

Robert F. Panara was born in the Upper Bronx of New York City. At the age of ten, he contracted spinal meningitis and became deaf. He was largely self-taught, reading his own books during classes at public schools because there were no notetakers or interpreters. After graduating from high school in 1938, he relocated with his family to Fall River, Massachusetts, where he found work at a clothing factory. Fortunately, he learned of Gallaudet College and applied. Dr. Percival Hall, the president of Gallaudet, realized that Panara did not know sign language and sent him to the American School for the Deaf in Hartford, Connecticut, for a postgraduate year before enrolling at Gallaudet in 1940.

After graduating in 1945, Panara accepted a position at the New York School for the Deaf, which had moved to White Plains but was still known as Fanwood, and there he began his legendary teaching career. After earning his master's degree from New York University in 1948, Panara taught at Gallaudet until he became the first Deaf professor at the National Technical Institute for the Deaf (NTID) in 1967, where he established its departments of English and Performing Arts. His scholarship broke ground in Deaf studies; he published many articles, coedited *Silent Muse: An Anthology of Poetry and Prose by the Deaf*, coauthored two books of biographies of deaf people, and served as an editor of the Gallaudet Encyclopedia of Deafness and Deaf People. Panara was always active in theater, both at Gallaudet and NTID, and he was a founding member of the National Theatre of the Deaf. After his retirement, NTID named its theater in his honor. Panara holds many awards and honors, including honorary doctorates from MacMurray College and Gallaudet. He is the subject of a biography by Harry Lang titled *Teaching from the Heart and Soul: The Robert F. Panara Story*.

On His Deafness

My ears are deaf, and yet I seem to hear
Sweet nature's music and the songs of man
For I have learned from Fancy's artisan
How written words can thrill the inner ear
Just as they move the heart, and so for me
They also seem to ring out loud and free.

In silent study I have learned to tell
Each secret shade of meaning and to hear
A magic harmony, at once sincere,
That somehow notes the tinkle of a bell,
The cooing of a dove, the swish of leaves,
The raindrop's pitter-patter on the eaves,
The lover's sigh, the thrumming of guitar,
And, if I choose, the rustle of a star!

Lip Service

You want to rap
you said
and let it all hang out
this thing about
the communication gap
that keeps us separate
your kind from mine.

You want to rap
you said
you want to integrate
but you decline
to change your line
of crap
from speech
to signs.

Idylls of the Green[*]
(College Days at Gallaudet)

I

Now that we are old and gray
and we live to pass the time,
let us look back at yesterday
when our youth was in its prime.
How can anyone forget
our "college daze" at Gallaudet
when we all were "Prepar-Rats"
with bow ties and mini-hats
proudly wearing "Buff and Blue"
(as General Washington did, too)!

II

Still preserved in memory
stands the Men's Refectory
where our "soap box" orator
led that old "Bean Song" encore—
"Beans, beans, the musical food,
the more you eat, the more you toot
the more you toot, the better you feel
so let's have beans with every meal!"

Oh, we surely had a ball
those weekday nights in College Hall!
Just to list a few digressions—
some guys plunged into "bull sessions"
(how they loved to "shoot the breeze"
clad only in their B.V.D.s!)
some would sing and sign-along

---

* Robert Panara wrote extensive notes to this poem to explain certain terms. His notes are found at the end of the poem.

to a ballad or a bawdy song;
some smoked pipes or cigarettes
or read a spicy French Gazette;
some gave poker games a whirl
and lose their "Varga pin-up girls";
but the pin-ups prized by one and all
were the ones locked up in Fowler Hall!

III

Speaking of the fairer sex,
social life was quite complex
since our gals were held in thrall
by those rules of Fowler Hall.
We would write those "K.O.B.s"
and implore their kisses, please—
"Kindness of the Bearer," aye,
they would surely make our day!

How those couples used to spoon
on a Sunday afternoon
when the sun was dropping slow
as they strolled down "Lovers' Row"!
And on "Sadie Hawkins Day"
every gal would vie to pay
for the hero of their dreams
and then treat him to ice creams.

But those pleasures had less merit
when they led to quick demerits,
thus we bowed (with tongue in cheek)
to the dictum of Miss Peet
who would warn her sweet young ladies:
"Holding hands will lead to babies!"

IV

If we hoped to stay in school
we had to obey the rules

lest we surely would inherit
those "black marks" they called demerits—
study hours after dinner
served to make us even thinner
so, from Seven to Nine
Proctors made us toe the line
(just the Preps and Frosh, of course,
and anyone who flunked a Course).

Then there was that Code of Dress
(kept us neat, I must confess)
coats expected of the guys
shirts all buttoned up, and ties;
skirts and blouses for the gals,
hairdos neatly done, et al.;
shoes, not sneakers, were the norm
once outside respective dorms.

Also published clear and loud
No Kind of Smoking was allowed;
as for liquor—what you think?
We knew how to smuggle (wink)!
These rules just never seemed to end,
they'd haunt us time and time again;
thus, as if those "black marks" were extended
to Twenty-five, you'd be suspended,
and if they totalled Thirty-five
you'd better kiss your books goodbye!

V

Yet, if these rules seemed rather stark,
life in college was a lark
with no captioned films or TV—
we had other ways to please thee,
weekend nights in Chapel Hall
served to occupy us all—
plays, and skits, and pantomimes,

classic poetry in sign;
and (as if we had to prove it)
we had dancing without music.
Simply clear the chairs away
and our feats were on display—
the fox trot, waltz, and "Lindy Hop,"
the jitterbug without a stop . . .
or, if just a Silent Movie
holding hands was just as "groovy"!

Oops! but I forgot to say
when we cleared those chairs away
someone had to put them back,
row on row, in perfect track.
This, we did, as was our duty,
with such speed, it was a beauty,
as we set the scene aright
for the Chapel talks on Sunday night.

Although these sometimes seemed a bore,
we did profit from them more
by gazing on in fascination
at each speaker's animation
because our Profs performed so well
in SimCom, Mime, and ASL.
Thus we learned, as imitators
to be skilled communicators!

VI

Ah! that was the golden age
when Tradition was the rage—
the "Coffin Door" that took a lickin'
but, like Timex, "kept on tickin',"
the "Mollycoddle" football game
when Thanksgiving morning came—
Preparats and Freshman versus
Upperclassmen (quite a circus)

with the Co-eds all cheerleading
and their heroes' noses bleeding!
The "Tug-O-War" in mud and slime;
the photo-shoots at Christmas time—
a "Currier and Ives" vignette
of Alice and Tom Gallaudet!
Oh, yes, of course—we must include
that sudden "Snow Bath" in the nude
and "dunking Seniors," at a whim
in the icy pool of dear "Ole Jim"!
In addendum, I must add
those other escapades we had—
the "Class Spreads" out on Hotchkiss Field
(what garlic scents it used to yield!);
those moonlight visits to the Farm
and secret trysts inside the Barn!

VII

Placed in Washington, D.C.,
there were many sights to see—
without ado, I'll name a few:
great Union Station, there to view
the "Iron Horses," old and new,
the Fountain of Columbus, too;
the trolley cars that, for a dime
conserved our purse at dating time
and, with "free transfers" to and fro,
they took us where we wished to go;
the Library of Congress, where
we snoozed while doing research there;
the statues all around the town
that honored persons of renown
and seemed to us their life-like looks
exceeded those in picture books.
Mt. Vernon, where we used to bike
in tandem on the Old Turnpike
(because of war-time rationing

we had no cars or gasoline);
the White House, the parades to view
on Pennsylvania Avenue;
the Tidal Basin in the spring
abloom with cherries blossoming;
the old Smithsonian where, mon Dieu,
they housed "The Spirit of St. Loo";
and, ah, the grandest sight of all—
the Washington and Lincoln Mall!
We soaked in all that history
and, better still, it was cost-free!

VIII

L'Envoi

I guess it's time to take the cue
and bid "the good old days" adieu,
but, as you very well can see,
in our book of memory
we retain each vivid scene
of "Life as Lived on Kendall Green."
That said, our little play is done
and so we take our leave, anon.

Panara's Notes

The Green: "Once fabled for its acres of luxuriant landscape and farm-lands, the campus at Gallaudet University is known as 'Kendall Green'—named after Amos Kendall, Postmaster General under Andrew Jackson, who generously donated several acres and its first building in 1856."

Prepar-Rats: "At Gallaudet College/University, the Preparatory Class is known as the lowly 'Rats.'"

Buff and Blue: "The college colors, also the colors derived from Gen. George Washington and his Continental Army, and still evident in the marble floor tiles in College Hall."

Men's Refectory: "Men's Dining Hall. Men and women had separate dining halls up until the expansion years of the late 1950s at Gallaudet."

K.O.B.s: "Men and women exchanged letters, love notes, etc., via 'K.O.B.s' or 'Kindness of Bearer' (usually the 'Head Seniors,' close friends, and/or schoolmates serving as unofficial campus mail)."

Demerits: "Although a carryover from the Victorian Era, Gallaudet maintained the system of handing out demerits ('black marks' or notations in the pocket notebooks carried by the Faculty members) to students who broke the rules. This procedure was somewhat arbitrary in allotment, depending on the mood of the Faculty-witness and how severe or flagrant the offense."

Miss Peet: Elizabeth Peet, from the Peet family famous for its long line of deaf and hearing educators and leaders, was the legendary dean of women.

Coffin Door: "Shaped like an upright coffin lid, this oaken relic was a side-door exit/entrance to College Hall (the men's dormitory) and the President's office on the ground floor. Thus, it was subject to the mood of the moment—a student exiting or entering in haste; leaving the Prexy's [President's] office after being called on the carpet; etc. Its age-old scars bear testimony to the many lickings it absorbed from assorted boot and shoe styles—as well as to its durability."

Tug-O-War: "Annual Thanksgiving Day rite on the west campus of 'Faculty Row,' pitting male Preps vs. Frosh while a forceful flow of water from a firehose separated the two sides—until, of course, the vanquished suffered a literal washout."

Snow Bath: "Starting with the first big snowfall, male students were carried naked to a big snowpile on the west campus and ceremoniously 'baptized.' Then they had to run back to the warmth of the dormitory, evading the tackles of a defensive line of upperclassmen comfortably dressed in winter jackets and boots. Fortunately, this rite took place at night, and its view was blocked by the dormitory from the sightlines of 'peeking Thomasinas' in adjacent Fowler Hall."

Dunking Seniors: "Another annual rite, a week or two before Graduation Day, when the underclassmen got revenge against the Seniors, who were rudely awakened from their deep dreams of peace and carried naked to the gymnasium (Ole Jim) where they were dunked into the unheated swimming pool."

Class Spreads: "End-of-each-trimester rite celebrated by classmates of both sexes, picnic-style, 'under the stars' or else separately in dormitories (usually including bootlegged 'moonshine')."

The Farm: "Up until the expansion era of the late 1950s, Gallaudet maintained a Farm where it raised cows, chickens, pigs, etc. This was a throwback to earlier days when a program in Agriculture was offered, usually for those students who came from large farming families and who expected to continue such career vocations back at home or elsewhere. It was also the ideal place to learn about 'the birds and the bees.'"

The Barn: "The most conspicuous (and popular meeting place) on the farm—a big red barn with haylofts!"

Ars Poetica

(Or, Advice to Aspiring Deaf Poets)

If you would be a poet, mark these words:
Most modern writers thrive on naked verbs
As readers dote on headlines. Never fear
The use of "free verse" when you cannot hear

Those cunning accents of our native tongue—
The poet is the master of the song,
And poetry depends as much on reason
As hunting deer, when only done in season.

Beware of metaphors that would revive
Those golden days when knighthood was alive—
You'll do much better, in this age atomic,
To write of mice and men gone supersonic,
Of chimpanzees aloft in guided missile,
And UFO's that still remain a puzzle.

And, if you still would search for Truth and Beauty,
Take care your sentiments are not too fruity
Nor look to Rome and Paris for finesse
But rather at their fashions of undress.
Be politics or cinema your theme,
The soul should seldom enter in the scene.
And, whether in Ivy League or in the slums,
Youth must be served by beating bongo drums.

And, last of all (and much to my regret,
I haven't been successful at it yet),
The secret's not so much in what you say
But how you say it—and then make it pay!

Mervin D. Garretson
(1923–)

MERVIN D. GARRETSON is the second modern poet, after Loy E. Golladay, to dedicate most of his art to Deaf themes, often using them bluntly as politically charged declarations and even as indictments. In "for Bill Stokoe," he portrays Deaf culture as being in the dark and lost before Stokoe sparked a controversy among linguists in the 1960s by arguing that the sign language of Deaf North Americans was not a broken version of English but a language in its own right. Although Deaf culture was very much alive, and many Deaf intellectuals instinctively knew the truth about their language, it was embattled, having been under siege by the oralists for generations. The grassroots Deaf population, however, did not feel so burdened. They rarely considered questions about who they were—they simply went about their business being themselves. So, for many generations, a chasm existed between the intellectuals who graduated from Gallaudet and those who went into trade work immediately after high school, most often in printing.

Garretson's "to Doin Hicks" is an appreciative glimpse into the "native wisdom" of the grassroots Deaf community and the lessons it offered to the white-collar Gallaudet alumni, including the creation of their own "atmosphere to be." Being an expert in the "field of deafness" himself, it is to Garretson's credit that he wrote "to an expert," a poem criticizing the myopia of colleagues out of touch with Deaf children as human beings. One can find the same spirit of assertion, this time expressed in a miniature narrative, in the poignant "deaf again," which makes manifest the intimate effects of oralism-audism—with all of the self-doubting it engenders in its victims—and, ultimately, its failure. After all, Deaf people, like the subject of this poem, have always and will always return to signing, to Deaf culture, and to their "home."

Mervin D. Garretson was born in Sheridan, Wyoming. He became deaf at five due to spinal meningitis. Because Wyoming had no programs for deaf children, Garretson attended the Colorado School for the Deaf and Blind. He entered the preparatory program at Gallaudet College in 1942. In 1947, he graduated from Gallaudet, married, and began teaching at the Maryland School for the Deaf. He accepted a teaching position at the Montana School for the Deaf and Blind (MSDB) in 1949, becoming principal of the Deaf department a year later. In 1953, he was divorced with two daughters. Two years later, Garretson married Carol Kaull, a colleague at MSDB.

Garretson received his master's degree in English with Phi Kappa Phi honors from the University of Wyoming. He became the first Deaf professor in the Graduate School at Gallaudet in 1962. Garretson's doctoral studies in English at the University of Maryland were abandoned in 1967 when he was hired as executive director of the Council of Organizations Serving the Deaf (COSD). He left COSD in 1970 to become the first principal of the Model Secondary School for the Deaf. From 1976 until his retirement in 1989, he worked in administration, serving as special assistant to four Gallaudet presidents (but not Elisabeth Zinser, whose appointment in 1988 sparked the Deaf President Now! Revolution). Garretson directed the first Deaf Way International Conference in 1989. Throughout his adult life, he was active in the National Association of the Deaf, editing *The Deaf American* and serving as president, and in the World Federation of the Deaf, serving for two decades as the chair of its Commission on Pedagogy. Garretson's collection of poetry, *words from a deaf child*, appeared in 1984.

for Bill Stokoe

i.

in other years our light burned low
o darkest night
sign hung up on the cross
verboten was the word
deaf as a culture lost
nothing we saw was heard

gone days of Milan smog*
careening in the fog
clods in a world of sound
clouds in a cloudless sky
mouthing like jesters crowned
questing the untold why

of life just one small part
a shadow of the whole
sign buried in the heart
language without a soul.

ii.

somewhere a lighthouse gleam
someone who dared to dream
a candle lit, a flame

---

* The Second International Congress on Education of the Deaf, which met at Milan, Italy, in 1880, passed resolutions against the use of sign language in schools for deaf children. One such resolution stated, "The Convention, considering the incontestable superiority of articulation over signs in restoring the deaf-mute to society and giving him a fuller knowledge of language, declares that the oral method should be preferred to that of signs in the education and instruction of deaf-mutes." Only the American delegates and one English delegate voted against the resolutions. Many in the signing community blamed the resolutions for the spread of oralism, but the reality is that the congress had little power over any changes in policy; rather, the 1880 resolutions merely reflected a direction that many educators were already determined to pursue.

soaring from mind to hand
a fire sparked by a name
that swept across our land

what's in this man, a cause
that seeks the are, not was
transfiguring night to day

with every newfound rule
facing the angry sway
of time and ridicule

we'll not forget the hour
he came to Gallaudet
the sun shone hope
the smog glowed stars.

to Doin Hicks

one Saturday evening not long ago
inveigled to see the "Billy Jack" show
    which I was told was captioned and all that
    but . . . shocked into a mental acrobat
I learned about the
    protoplasmic
              psychopastic
                  too elastic
properties of cow turd
told by some genius bird
from Miz-Arkansas way
in a western roundelay

delivered faultlessly with tongue-in-cheek
a signarama fit to beat the Greek
tragedies of Aeschylus and Lisistrae
a comic-tragedy that is to say
from one nursed
well-versed in forensic art
the next rhyme is tempting but I'll not start
reverting back again to protoplasm
there's a limit to iconoclasm!

at any rate it's time for me to share
with you and Wanda all my thanks—a rare
and glorious night in June it was for me
    with friends
    in warmth
    and atmosphere to be.

to an expert

with your psychometrics charts and tables
graphs and lines you geographize
a vicarious silence
your maps
paper journeys
across the highways of deafness
with your test tubes antiseptic laboratories
audiology and audiometrics
language and speech and speech and language
far from the vital spark
locked in your sterile cloister
yours the definition but not the meaning
yours the sound the look of life
mine the sight the feel
when will you learn
as you skim across the surface
when will you know
as you travel along
each country and each city
each lowly street
has a soul.

deaf again

he was a deaf teacher of deaf children
at the Mary Magdalene Oral School
a deaf professional, proudly he taught
in his shining patent leather shoes
his grey pin-striped suit, paying his dues,
hiding behind his insecure deaf smile
in his ultra-oral environment.

sometimes he did find himself excluded
from conversation he could not hear
but that wasn't intentional, you understand.
they didn't really expect him to grasp
all that was said, you know, but he was there
and sometimes he wondered, were they aware?

he was all alone after school, of course,
(indoors he's deaf, and just as deaf outdoors!)
a neat piece of furniture, branch of a tree?
was he trying to seem instead of be?
but he was doing a great job of teaching
at the Mary Magdalene Oral School
a great job of reaching each little child.
a good oral model, no bystander,
he served without fuss, the great pretender!

he resigned last week . . . we wonder why?
back to the liberating world of sign,
where no one had to rationalize,
no more vacant, apologetic eyes,
no more somber suits, no more sick smile,
no more being polite, mouthing all the while!
no more parading in shirt, tie, and coat
and no more trying not to rock the boat.

ask him why . . . ask him why . . .
and he'll say:
never again, if again
live again, deaf again,
back again to life.
whole again, back again
home again, Deaf again, home.

Dorothy Miles
(1931–1993)

AT THE TIME DOROTHY MILES produced her book-and-video collection of written and signed poems, *Gestures*, the signing community was giving itself more and more permission to express art in its own language. Until William C. Stokoe's academic defense of American Sign Language (ASL) as a language in its own right, "signed" poetry was in the main recitations of written poems. Miles's work in the mid-1970s was a step away from this and a precursor to the ASL poetry revolution a decade later. Instead of performing written poems, she created poems with both writing and signing in mind—neither translations of written poems in ASL nor creations of ASL poems completely free of any thought of the printed word, but something in the middle. This paralleled the wide popularization of the Total Communication approach, which was then occurring in Deaf education.

After the decades-long stranglehold of oralism on the field, signing was finally brought back in the classroom, but it arrived politely and with assurances that it could coexist with what many hearing teachers and parents wanted to see: speaking and lip-reading. However, speaking and signing at the same time, a central tool of Total Communication known colloquially as Sim-Com, did not work very well because it compromised both languages—the spoken English got muddled, and the ASL lost its full expressive power. Aside from breaking some ground in cross-lingual poetics, Miles's work did not succeed for the same reason, at least not until after she returned to the United Kingdom and contributed greatly to research in British Sign Language (BSL) and did her poetry separately between written pieces and sign creations. Nevertheless, her "The Hang-Glider" is an apt allegory of "taking the leap" into the Deaf world. This poem, then, is a fine period piece;

the beginnings of the Deaf Pride movement saw the community, on all levels, taking flight.

Dorothy Miles was born in North Wales. During World War II, she was deafened by spinal meningitis. Miles attended a school in Manchester, where she received training in speech and learned a limited sign language used by the students, known as the "Manchester version." In 1946, she enrolled at England's first high school for deaf students, Mary Hare Grammar. In 1957, Miles went to America, drawn to Gallaudet College and the chance to become an actress. She "fell in love with American Sign Language," which she said was "so much more complete and creative" than BSL. Miles toured with the National Theatre of the Deaf and in 1976 published *Gestures: Poetry in American Sign Language*. She returned to England and worked as a social worker with young Deaf people in Uxbridge, as a researcher for the British Deaf Association and Interpreter Training Council, and as a contributor to a monumental dictionary of BSL. After her death, friends established in Guildford the Dorothy Miles Culture Centre to foster theater, poetry, and love of sign language among Deaf and hearing people alike. A larger collection of Miles's work was published posthumously as *Bright Memory*.

The Hang-Glider

Here are my wings;
And there, at the edge of nothing,
    wait the winds
to bear my weight.
My wings,
so huge and strong,
built with my life in mind . . .

I have made other wings before,
    test-tried,
                    wrong-broken,
                        cast aside—
I searched, and asked, and saw,
    and built again . . .
and here I stand.

Take up my courage
    with my pack,
and forward go—

    NO TURNING BACK!

(The wings won't turn.)

The cliff is high,
    and far way down
                the sea;
I'd hate to drown!

But they are watching me.

I have seen others do it—
    step off and fly—
so why can't I?

Suppose . . .
    suppose the winds might die
and I
    step off and dive

                and dive
                   and dive . . .

The winds won't die!
Experience tells me that.
Courage
and faith in my experience,
that's all I need.

Here are my wings . . .
Here are my wings.

Linwood Smith
(1943–1982)

LINWOOD SMITH DIED at the age of thirty-nine and, so, was denied the opportunity to fully mature as a poet. As a result, many of his poems seem to fall short of expressing all that he wished to say. Still, and perhaps even in part because they are neither developed nor sophisticated, they are profound. "Percy" and "Mike" are rare candid snapshots of Deaf children at school. The one shows the important role teachers play as surrogate parents, stepping in here and there when students' parents are absent, literally and figuratively. The other reveals many things, two of which are students' penchant for learning almost in spite of the classroom environment and the severe alienation many Deaf children felt, and continue to feel today, toward their uncommunicative parents. Deaf readers of a certain age will relate to "The Dream Song of a Deaf Man," which is about the ache of separation that was so absolute in the days before portable telephone devices for the Deaf, relay services, pagers, and video phones allowed long-distance communication.

Linwood Smith was born in Lumberton, North Carolina, and became deaf at the age of two. He earned his bachelor's degree from Gallaudet College in 1965 and his master's degree with the National Leadership Training Program at California State University at Northridge in 1971. Smith taught at Governor Morehead School for the Deaf and Blind and worked as a guidance counselor at the North Carolina School for the Deaf at Morganton before becoming coordinator of the National Center for Law and the Deaf at Gallaudet. A collector of books and pipes, he made significant contributions to the signing community, especially in mental health and Black Deaf culture. Smith served on many organization boards, as an editor, as president of Capital City

Association of the Deaf and the Washington, D.C., chapter of the Gallaudet College Alumni Association, and as a widely published writer. He authored *Silence, Love, and Kids I Know: Poems* (1979) and coauthored *Black and Deaf in America: Are We That Different?* (1983), still the definitive text on Black Deaf history and community. He was working as an educational specialist in a program serving mentally ill and emotionally disturbed Deaf youths and adults at Saint Elizabeths Hospital in Washington, D.C., when he was killed by a drunk driver.

Percy

Knowing full well he couldn't hear me
I whispered in his ear and walked away,
And like the cat that was killed by curiosity
He came to me and asked, "What was that you told
me yesterday?"
I signed "haircut."
He smiled and frowned, then said, "OK!"
Neat hair too is a source of pride
But the thing that made him do it was
he knew I cared . . .
and when he left . . . a part of me died
and a part of me cried for joy.

Mike

He never wanted to study.
Not because he didn't want to learn,
Or because he couldn't hear
But because he wanted to draw.
Every day he'd come to me
and say, "Can I draw?"
And I'd say, "No, it's time to read."
Then he'd open his notebook and show me his pictures . . .
Big, black, beautiful lines and circles that
I didn't understand.
Once I asked him, "What's that?" and he would flip the pages,
and explain, "That's Paul, that's Peter, that's Job
and that's the rope that Judas used to hang himself."
and he said, "Remember two weeks ago we studied the Bible?"
"Were you listening, you didn't seem to be paying attention,
I think I got you about ten times for daydreaming."
The bell rang, he smiled and left.
The next morning . . . like always . . .
"Can I draw today?"
And I said, "Sit down, Mike!"
After class, he came over laid five pictures on my desk
and said, "That's me, that's you, that's my father,
that's my mother, and that's God." and walked out.
Mike had a halo, I had wings, God had a beard,
His mother and father . . . were hanging from ropes.

The Dream Song of the Deaf Man

Under all speech that is good for anything there lies a silence
that is better.
—Thomas Carlyle

                         Because I'm here and
you are   far away
               and cannot visualize my
restless hands
moving inwards and outwards into space saying that in so many ways . . .
               I Love You.
               Because our ears weren't made for telephones
               and lonely nights and endless days
               have led our thoughts through a
               dark, vast maze
               to teach us the definition of
               Separation.
Because of all these things I send you this . . . Dream Song.
               Because each fleeting split second adds
another slither of pain to my sensitive heart, while tears fall
               jet-propelled
                    in
                    a
               thankless tempo
offering neither sympathy nor recompense for your absence.

Because the dawn stars far above are deaf to human pleas
and cannot understand
the foreign language of my hands
My state of mind made me send you this . . . Dream Song.
               Because my mute, aphonic lips
               can barely utter words of love
               and after my futile passionate pantomime

of how much to me you mean,
in the soundless night no answer comes
from your soft, sonic hands
to satisfy the dark, moonless void of the shores of space
within my heart.
                    And now, while all is the same as you and I
                    mute
                            as

                            a

                            meteor streaking through the night,
                    I send you my love
                    within this . . .
                            Dream Song.

Curtis Robbins
(1943–)

THE DEAF PRIDE MOVEMENT reached its zenith in March 1988 when the students and faculty of Gallaudet University, joined by practically the whole signing community, protested against the board of trustees' selection of a hearing woman, over two other Deaf finalists, for the school's next president. The triumph of the Deaf President Now! Revolution inspired many to write celebratory poems, but Curtis Robbins's "The Rally That Stood the World Still" includes another element, some nagging questions. Though the movement made vital breakthroughs for all Deaf people, it was by no means full reparation for past injustices, certainly not the pain of wrongs done by one's own family, a classic example of which is masterfully carved in "Solo Dining While Growing Up." In "The Promised World," Robbins lists the cultural bargains he has been offered, not only the age-old one to speak and act hearing, but also the new ideal Deaf identity, with which he finds himself at odds, too. Two of his lines—"Every chamber is loaded but one" ("Russian Roulette") and "I am lost" ("Deaf Poet or What?")—reveal how stuck some Deaf people can feel when they find employment opportunities still limited, even after the advent of the Americans with Disabilities Act, and when the current lexicon of labels doesn't fit them. In spite of it all, Robbins's art is uniquely commanding, clear, and pulls with much strength.

Curtis Robbins became deaf when he was one year old due to the side effects of a drug used to treat his tonsillitis. He attended public schools in New York City and Long Beach. Robbins graduated from Gallaudet College in 1967 and earned his master's degrees from New York University and the University of Maryland, where he also received his doctorate. He has taught computer applications and American Sign Language for more than thirty-five years. Robbins's poetry has appeared in the anthologies *Beyond Lament: Poets of the World Witness to the Holocaust*, *No Walls of Stone*, *The Deaf Way II Anthology*, and *Blood to Remember*.

The Rally That Stood the World Still

Our dried voices, when
We whisper together
Are quiet and meaningless
As wind and dry grass . . .

Remember us—if at all—not as lost
Violent souls, but only
As the hollow men
The stuffed men.
—T. S. Eliot

I stood wondering – among the excited crowd –
letting the world know the time has come –
if all the commotion would ever materialize.
Not that I had no confidence in the significance
of the intent – I'd just be fooling myself. I
just wondered if the world has been more deaf than it
was willing to admit – would it be worth it at all?

I stood wondering – among the quiet hands
screaming at the world to be heard –
if all the shouting could be seen. I was so
numb with confusion – the reality –
two deaf men and a hearing woman. And
there stood this other hearing woman announcing
to the world – not that the lady won –
that deaf people are not ready to function in
a hearing society. She wasn't either in the deaf.

I stood wondering – among the angry crowd –
whether the world might know that the time has come –
if all the commotion was worth it at all. Indeed!
Indeed, for all the misanthropic wisdom the

hearing world had about deaf people, then the demand
for a Deaf President Now was justified. It was
another shot heard around the world. It was
a time the world listened – for a change!

Solo Dining While Growing Up

When my whole family sat down at the dinner table:

There was always
                a lot to eat from corner to corner
There was always conversation
                between forks and spoons

There was always conversation
                between glasses and cups

There was always conversation
                between napkins

There were always
                empty plates and empty bowls

But the knife that laid between them all—
                from mouth to ear—
                      from mouth to eye—

                                          cut me off.

The Promised World

I nearly was born
   without hearing a sound
      and was promised the world
         with things to come
            if I had adapted—
                     imitating
       sound.

I was tutored with sound
    and was promised the world
       if I learned to deal
         with the hearing aid—
           thinking and believing
              I'm hearing everything—
          only to ask where and
              what they were.

I was raised
    and was promised the world
       if I behaved
         as if I didn't know
           the difference—
         only to wonder why.

I was educated at Gallaudet
    and was promised the world
       if I learned ASL
         and believe in the future
           scintillating on a silver platter—
              if only I heard beforehand.

I was raised
    to think and reason
        like a man—
            and was promised the world
                that I'd be a better man—
                if only they knew.

Russian Roulette

Every chamber is loaded but one.

I've written letters to a lot of employers
who have advertised about
available positions
and if interested apply.

It was worth trying, or so I thought.
It sounded so ideal
so perfect
so definitive
so excited—in fact,
too good to be true.

I waited
and waited
and waited
and waited.
The ad said not to call.
week after week
I waited
and waited
and waited.

It seems that none of bullet holes
on my resume
struck a chord.

Typically, my qualifying deafness
left them with a bang.

Deaf Poet or What?

They keep asking the same question:

"Are you a Deaf poet
Or
A Poet who is deaf?"

I shudder at the question.
I can't even think of a better way
to express the rhetoric.
I'm lost.

Did I mention anything otherwise?
Did I falter at my wordsmithing?
Did I recant from something so obvious?
Did I wreak poetic havoc?
Who am I?

or rather
What am I?

"Do you sign?"
Or
"Do you sing?"
Or
"Do you truly hear such peripatetic words?"

The matter doesn't warrant an answer—
I am what you read.

Clayton Valli
(1951–2003)

CLAYTON VALLI'S GLIDING AND eye-widening "A Dandelion" is, hands down, the signing community's best-loved American Sign Language (ASL) poem. It has been watched on video many times over and recited with much relish and pathos. Like many of his contemporaries who pioneered the art form, Valli thought for many years that his work could not be translated into English. How could something so beautiful and so powerful in its native airspace be harnessed on paper, in mere words?

One suspects this skepticism toward translation arose from a mistrust of the English language that many Deaf people share, partly because many of them themselves are not fully literate in it and are unable to be moved by words in the same ways literate readers can be moved. Another factor is the relative lack of literary interaction between ASL poets and fluent signers who have an intimate knowledge of poetry in both languages. But once Valli met and read Raymond Luczak's poetry, he took what he called a risk and let Luczak translate his most famous poem and another poem, "Pawns."

The results convinced Valli that ASL poetry could be translated after all. Something, as is always the case, is lost in translation, but it is good enough and does literature a great service. Unfortunately, these two poems were the only translations of Valli's work that he approved before he died. One important reason the two translations are a success is that Luczak is the same kind of poet in English that Valli was in ASL: a formalist, someone who plumbs artistic force from working within strict structures. Valli was the first to develop a kind of taxonomy of ASL poetry, replete with its equivalents of the line, rhyme, and other parameters, and, unlike some others, his feet stayed on the same spot so the camera angle need not move at all, letting his hands write within the frames.

Clayton Valli was born deaf in Seabrook, New Hampshire. After graduating from the Austine School for the Deaf in Vermont, he went to the National Technical Institute for the Deaf, where he earned an associate degree in photography. When he learned the Gunners needed a signing photographer to help in their work teaching the chimpanzee Washoe sign language, he applied and got the job. In Nevada, Valli also studied social psychology and received his bachelor's degree in 1978.

Discovering on his own a way to express poetry in pure ASL rather than mere approximations of English verse in signs, Valli became fascinated with linguistics, which he studied at Gallaudet, securing his master's degree in 1985. He then designed his own doctoral studies in linguistics and ASL poetics at Union Institute in Cincinnati, where he received his PhD in 1993. Valli performed his poetry and presented on sign language poetry worldwide, becoming easily the best-loved poet in any sign language. In addition to many scholarly publications and best-selling textbooks on ASL linguistics, Valli made two video collections of his poetry, one produced by Sign Media Inc., and the other by DawnSignPress, still available today. A victim of AIDS, he died of health complications. His sign memoir, "Poetry Exploding from the Heart" (a reference to the way the word "poetry" is signed, the fist representing the heart opening or "exploding" into the sign for "expression"), translated by Raymond Luczak, appeared in John Lee Clark's anthology *Clayton: A Tribute to Clayton Valli.*

A Dandelion

Translated from American Sign Language by Raymond Luczak

Their yellows dotted the field,
their petals waving with the breezes.

An irritated man stared at them, snarling,
"Dandelions!" His hands pulled
some apart, and mowed the rest down
until the field was smoothed out
in green. The rain soon came
and went away; the sun sneaked in,
warming a seed in the soil.
The seed rose, enjoying all nature.

It waved, watching a bee
coming by with a greeting and
going away. Nights it closed
its petals, opening up again
in the morning. One day it turned
into white puffs, their whiskers
a halo, but it still moved with the breeze.
Its seedlings flew off in every direction.

Spotting its whiteness, the man,
enraged, spit out, "There!"
The brave white puff still waved,
still sending off its seedlings.
The man grabbed its stem and pulled out.
The white puff exploded, its seedlings
scattering everywhere on its own.

Pawns

Translated from American Sign Language by Raymond Luczak
in memory of John D. Smith and Sam Edwards

On the neat black-and-white squares of land,
The Kings, Queens, Bishops and their horses
Stood in their own castles, quibbling and quibbling
About nothing. At last they agreed and looked over
Their not-so-important pawns to be taken away
Ruthlessly. Stunned, the pawns all gathered around
In private for support and exchange of needs.

Yet in their midst, one by one they died.
The pawns went up to the Kings, Queens, and Bishops
To try, desperately, reasoning with them.
They were lost in their own world, still quibbling
And quibbling among themselves about nothing.
The pawns rallied each other for support,
But still one by one of their own died.

One of them on one side was a Deaf friend
With a colorful skull cap, a stud earring, and a moustache
Expressing peacefully, "Death is beautiful."
One of them on the other side was a Deaf friend
With purple-dyed hair, a sleeveless shirt, and a moustache
Saying joyfully, "Life is beautiful."

From both sides their lives immortalized
In quilts revealing their names: Sam Edwards and John D. Smith.
Their quilts joined with many others on the lawn
While files of people streamed past ghosts,
Mingling death and life. How beautiful.

The Kings, Queens, Bishops, and horses still quibbled,
In their castles with their flags, about nothing.
The pawns ceased trying to fight with them,
Looking instead at the flags on both sides waving.

A Deaf pawn came forth and began signing
those star-spangled banners,
so beautiful and high . . .
Shall they all be stitched into the quilts, too?

Is that so beautiful?

E. Lynn Jacobowitz
(1953–)

ASSERTING, AS MANY AMERICAN Sign Language (ASL) poets do, that her poem "cannot be translated," E. Lynn Jacobowitz advises her readers to "please use [their] imagination and sign along in a slow, rhythmic form." Yet her notes for the signs and facial expressions used in "In Memoriam: Stephen Michael Ryan" go a long way in evoking in text some of the poem's power. Imagination is needed to appreciate any translation, but since the gloss stops short of translation, some knowledge of ASL is required for a fair appreciation. Jacobowitz uses the signing community's most popular formal storytelling scheme, narrating only with the handshapes representing the English alphabet and in its order. As some of these handshapes are rarely used beyond fingerspelling English words, it is a remarkable accomplishment to use them—only one-third of the total handshapes available in ASL—smoothly, without any awkwardness. The signing reader will find Jacobowitz's selections for signs in this poem especially fine, but the nonsigning reader will still get a sense of the poem's poignant frankness mixed with tenderness.

E. Lynn Jacobowitz was born in Brooklyn, New York. At eight months, she became deaf after contracting spinal meningitis. Before entering Gallaudet College in 1971, she attended the Lexington School for the Deaf and New Utrecht High School without graduating. Jacobowitz received a bachelor's degree in psychology and creative learning from Gallaudet and later earned her master's degree in education communication from the University of Maryland in 1981. After teaching two years at Delgado Junior College in New Orleans, she began her long career in 1979 as professor in the Department of Sign Communication (now the Department of American Sign Language and Deaf Studies) at Gallaudet.

Jacobowitz has been active in many organizations, including the powerful American Sign Language Teachers Association, where she has served as vice president and president, and currently is the chair of two committees. In 2001, she earned a doctorate in administration and supervision in higher education from Gallaudet. She is also involved with the Maryland School for the Deaf, where she coaches soccer and basketball, which both of her daughters play.

In Memoriam: Stephen Michael Ryan

A: Drinking-beer (alternate hands)
B: Beer (repeat twice)
C: Beer belly
D: Tall
    ~pause for 5 seconds~
E: Signing (use both hands simultaneously)
F: Storytelling (repeat twice)
G: Peabrain?
H: Funny?
I: Idea (with assured look)
J: Imaginative (with assured look)
K: Visual (lean forward in emphasis for 5 seconds)
L: Laughing (circular)
    ~pause for 5 seconds~
M: Rolling with laughter (slow motion)
N: Humorous (repeat twice)
    ~pause for 5 seconds~
O: Going home (slow motion)
P: Passed-out (sudden motion)
Q: Feel-pulse-on neck
    Feel-pulse-on wrist
R: Realize (with frightened look)
S: Stephen heart-beating (slower and slower)
T: Heart-stopped (handshape is different, STOP)
    ~pause for 5 seconds~
U: Lying down in a coffin (with sad look)
V: Funeral viewing (repeat with sad and sadder looks)
W: Cremated (lying position then on body)
X: Cry (show a tear on face)
Y: Pour-ashes (move the other hand for Avon-by-the-Sea,
    Gallaudet,
    Seattle, and
    Giants Football Stadium)

Z: Point to his ashes (slowly ascending to the heavens)
    ~ pause for 5 seconds ~

A: Daughter-girl (look at Erin Ryan)
B: Son-boy (look at Sean Ryan)
C: Wife (look at Laureen)
D: Lonely (use other hand to point at the three of them)
E: Signing (look at Stephen)
F: Storytelling (look at Stephen, then at the audience)
G: Peabrain (nod with affirmative expression)
H: Funny (nod with affirmative expression)
    ~ pause for 5 seconds ~
I: Ego (look at Stephen, sign emphatically)
K: Look-up-to (look at Stephen, sign proudly)
L: Laugh, Sad-lips (sign laugh, then change to sad lips)
M: Sad-lips (both hands show lips drooping downward)
    ~ pause for 5 seconds ~
N–O: No no no no (as if Stephen signs it vigorously)
P: Look-down-on-you (as if Stephen looks at us)
Q: Peabrain (as if Stephen insults us)
R: Reason (as if Stephen uses a rhetorical, self-explanatory
    question)
S: Stephen kiss-fist (as if Stephen tries to explain to us that he is
    Stephen and everyone loves him)
T: Against sad-lips (as if Stephen tries to tell us that he is against
    our sadness)
U: Funny (as if Stephen tells us that he is funny and he wants us
    to remember his funniness)
    ~ pause for 5 seconds ~
V: Look-up (we look up to Stephen with a smile)
W: Cherish (sign with sentimental feeling)
X: Determination (show vigorously)
Y: Party, drinking, fooling-around (show our happy spirits)
Z: Memory-etched-on mind
    Tear-on face
    Smile-on mouth

Debbie Rennie
(1957–)

THE YEAR 1980 WAS VERY EXCITING for Deaf theater as Mark Medoff's *Children of a Lesser God* won the Tony Award for best play. Phyllis Frelich, who played Sarah Norman, won the Tony Award for best actress, then the highest honor conferred on a Deaf actor. Marlee Matlin later won an Oscar for the same role in the 1986 film adaptation. The signing community became ambivalent about Matlin the following year when, at the Academy Awards, she voiced her speech before fingerspelling the names of the nominees for an award. While Sarah Norman jutted her jaw defiantly at oralism, Matlin broke character, divorcing herself from the role model the character had become.

Debbie Rennie wrote her poem "As Sarah" before the Matlin controversy tainted how many signers saw the movie. Rennie played the role in a 1985 stage production by the National Technical Institute for the Deaf (NTID). In her marvelously compact poem, she not only tells us that she identifies with the character, but she slips into it, almost as if she is writing it "as Sarah." Therefore, it is a true actor's poem in which the reader learns more about the character than the actor. Also, it is an example of the foreigner's grasp of English with which many Deaf people write, the same manner in which Sarah Norman would have written, unpolished but loud and clear.

Debbie Rennie was born deaf ("It was a big gift!") in Erie, Pennsylvania, to hearing parents, and she has a deaf brother. She graduated from the Western Pennsylvania School for the Deaf and was drawn to New York, where she learned dance and performed professionally. Studying under the great Deaf actors Patrick Graybill and Howie Seago at NTID, she earned her bachelor of fine arts degree from Rochester Institute of Technology and also a master's degree in arts education.

In 1981, she toured with NTID's award-winning theater group Sunshine Too and also was instrumental in the founding of Bridge Of, an American Sign Language poetry performing group that included Jim Cohn, Kenny Lerner, and Peter Cook. Since 1988, Rennie has lived in Sweden, teaching theater and performing all over Europe. She is married to the Deaf artist Peter Zacsko, and they have two adopted daughters, one from India and one from China.

As Sarah

I played her
because she drew a hearing aid on
a picture of Virgin Mary
Her mother cried and
threw her out to deaf school
she thought that her own daughter is
mental retarded.
I understand her very well
She filled up with rage inside her
Again, mother wants her to be normal by
fucking with hearing boys.

Willy Conley
(1958–)

"A DEAF BAPTISM," Willy Conley's clever miniature parable, pays respects to Hans Christian Andersen's famous ugly duckling, here representing someone who is plunged into the Deaf world. The poem is a member of a long line of works in Deaf literature and artwork featuring birds. One needs only to look elsewhere in this book to find other examples, including Raymond Luczak's "Hummingbirds" and Christopher Jon Heuer's "Bone Bird." Birds lend themselves well to metaphor and symbolism in general, but what makes them more attractive for literary use by Deaf artists is the imagery of wings, which represents hands flying in the air.

"The Miller of Moments" is another almost purely photographic snapshot of a poem. It is more layered and it fairly sings in its appreciation of the miracle of Deaf theater's existence, remarkable not only for what is performed but also for being performed at all. Given that the business of theater is already difficult, it is even more challenging for such a small community.

"Salt in the Basement" is among a growing body of literature written in "ASL style," following American Sign Language grammar instead of English. Deaf writers have long been experimenting with how to represent ASL dialogue, especially since the publication in 1986 of the first novel by a Deaf writer starring Deaf characters, *Islay* by Douglass Bullard. David Anthony published in 1992 a widely read article in *The Deaf American* written entirely in this manner. While other items, such as Luczak's short story "Poster Child" and Sara Stallard's series of flash memoirs "OJ & PJ," are in "prose" ASL gloss, Conley is the first, after Loy E. Golladay's two mediocre attempts, to succeed in doing this in a poem.

Willy Conley was born profoundly deaf in Baltimore, where he attended public schools, always the only deaf student. In 1976, he entered Rochester Institute of Technology where he received his bachelor's degree in biomedical photography. It was there that he first learned ASL, began writing, and fell in love with theater. After graduation, he worked for seven years in medical centers at Yale, Johns Hopkins, the University of Texas, and Cedars-Sinai in Los Angeles as a medical photographer. Then he left the medical profession, though not photography, and performed with several touring theater companies, most notably the National Theatre of the Deaf (NTD).

Upon learning that most of the plays that NTD produced were written by hearing playwrights, Conley decided to study playwriting at Boston University, with Nobel laureate Derek Walcott, and at Towson University, where he earned his master of fine arts degree. Since then, over a dozen of his plays have been produced, and many of them have been published in *Vignettes of the Deaf Character and Other Plays* (2009). Conley is the chair of the Theater Arts Department at Gallaudet University and lives in Hanover, Maryland, with his wife Stella and their son, Clayton Lee.

A Deaf Baptism

A family of Mallards
near a waterfall's green ledge
paddling
preening
shivering off waterbugs
A feather or two comes loose
and floats over the water's edge

Suddenly a duckling
chasing after a feather
flapping
jerking
toppling over the waterfall
lost it struggles through
the curtain into the world of white water

The Miller of Moments

on Pattaconk Brook
in Chester, Connecticut
up in a little tower
above the old grist mill

someone
steams rain
sifts thunder
sews lightning
squeezes sunlight
saves sign language

a pair of hands
open the wood slats

the flowers hold their scents
the brook ceases babbling
the ivy stops crawling
the wind looks back

eyes for darkness
watches below
the daily struts and frets
of drama school deaf actors
their private moments

when the sun
bows to the horizon
the hands withdraw

come morning the summer school cook
rips yesterday off the calendar
before people walk in and out
for three squares a day

no one notices
the yearly scores
of faint footprints
up on the mill tower deck

yet another day
the spirit of Deaf Theatre
survives

Salt in the Basement

An American Sign Language Reverie in English

me little, almost high wash-wash machine
down basement, me have blue car
drive drive round round
basement

happen summer time
me inside blue car
drive round round
basement

me drive every corner
drive drive drive
then BOOM! me crash

there brown paper round tall
me get out car
look inside brown round tall
many many small small
white rock rock
small white rock rock

for-for?

me put white rock rock
in mouth
very very salty
same-same Grandma
mashed-mashed potato

me again sit blue car
drive round round
basement

happen winter
father down basement
go to brown round tall
father shovel big lump
there white rock rock
many white rock rock

father told me for-for
outside road

me ask again for-for?

me outside blue car, cold cold
drive drive straight straight
me watch father

white rock rock father throw throw
on walk-walk
father his brown car
throw white rock rock
throw round throw round

me ask father for-for?

father say for mother
white rock rock for mother?

me get off blue car
me look down white rock rock
burn burn hole many many
hole in ice
same-same ice my lemon drink

me jaw-drop
white rock rock
make hole in ice break-break
same-same make hole in my tummy?

that why me pee-pee
poo-poo always?

me no more eat
white rock rock
down basement

me remember
mother year past
happen winter
mother outside
ice all-over
mother fall
arm broke

father told me
go down basement
stay stay
me inside blue car
drive round round
basement

Peter Cook
(1962–)

MOST AMERICAN SIGN LANGUAGE (ASL) poetry, interestingly, is universal, not Deaf, in content. When Deaf poets create work in their native language, they are likely to be much less conscious of their "otherness" than are Deaf poets who write in English. In other words, it is as fundamental human beings—citizens of the world—that ASL poets express their art. Another way to understand this is that poetry articulated in ASL is automatically Deaf and, therefore, does not need to be explicitly Deaf.

It is intriguing, then, to find ASL poets' occasional forays into more readily addressing the Deaf experience. The signing stylist Peter Cook's two written poems here are examples of this general rule, and even though his pieces in the Flying Words Project section do touch on deafness, they are exceptions that prove the rule that very little ASL poetry is Deaf in content. Cook's two poems here deal with questions of truth and language. Mainstream society uses language to define what is true, but thanks to Cook's deafness and oralist background, the spell does not quite work on him; as a result, he is able to gleefully say "the truth does not lie to me."

Peter Cook was born in Parkersburg, West Virginia, and became deaf at the age of three due to spinal meningitis. His parents sent him to Clarke School for the Deaf, a staunchly oralist program. In the ninth grade, he transferred to Selebury, a private school where he was the only deaf student. He did not learn ASL until he auditioned for a play at the National Technical Institute for the Deaf and got a part that required ignorance of ASL. After six months among signing actors, Cook became a signing stylist and began to perform his own creative work.

Since graduating with a bachelor's degree in graphic design, he has taught at Columbia College, where he received the 1997 Excellence in Teaching Award, and elsewhere while performing internationally with Kenny Lerner under the rubric of the Flying Words Project. He appeared on PBS's *United States of Poetry* and has performed at many festivals, including the Deaf Way II International Cultural Arts Festival and the Tales of Graz in Austria. He lives in Chicago.

Don Quoxitie Didnt Really Attack the Windmill*

he never attack the windmill
i shall prove it with my wooden shoes on
doing some cola on rust
it's in the book that said he did.
but book is a book; i saw in my own eyes
don't get me wrong, i'm deaf and truth can't lie to me
wanna know the stuff, the right stuff?
just look at those federal kids brawling in the
great fueless heated cone house.
sir, have you make any progress?
yes, with a snicker in the corner of mouth
oh . . you mean that all problems is over?
well, ya know, it's in the paper now, don't worry man.
oh . . is the lybian problem over?
    russian over?
    south African over?
    deficit over?
    environment over?
snicker still there . . Don Quoxitie didn't really attack . . .

---

* The spelling in this poem is intentional, reflecting the way fingerspelling tends to approximate English words rather than spelling them out to the last letter.

Ringoes

Only thing I could remember was
smell of August humid tall grasses in
beam of the afternoon sun.
It was sunday.
I knew it because I did not have to sit
on the pew and play tic, tac, and toe with my dad.

Ron was the only boy I could play with
because God have all angels on this days.
and I did not feel bad.

I knew God watch them in their mon-sat mischief.

Ron, reach out for my shoulder

tap

tap

tap

As I turn around,

Ron's teeth seemed to close tight and smile
without raising his eyebrows.
His teeth wide opened and I could see his tongue
touched the frontal teeth, then snapped back to the
back of his mouth, and his apple in his turtleneck
sweater shook rapidly.

Only thing I understand was fear in his eyes.

I focused on where his path of eyes
aimed at:
Three crawling garter snakes
acting as climbing vines among
tall grasses of my own backyard.

A mind editing image flashed in my head;
a teacher holding a picture card of a green snake
next to her mouth.
She did what Ron did to me:

SSS NAAEE K

She pointed to the picture.
She did again what Ron did to me.

SSS NAAEE K

She did repeat with the picture until I become her
dog: I nodded my head.

All I know that snakes have tiny tongues
but what it got have do with ss naaee k?

Flying Words Project: Peter Cook and Kenny Lerner (est. 1984)

THE FLYING WORDS PROJECT has met, and continues to meet, with wide acclaim both in the signing community and the mainstream. It does not pretend to translate the American Sign Language (ASL) poetry that Peter Cook performs. Even if full and nuanced translations were done, they could scarcely be presented to audiences at the same time as the signed performances. Instead, Cook's collaborator, Kenny Lerner, speaks what can only be described as "captions" to what is happening on the stage. The captions are supplementary, mere suggestions and hints for nonsigners as to what artistic heights are unfolding before their untrained eyes. Nonsigners know immediately that Cook is expressing much more than what is spoken, and because the spoken English takes a backseat, they can begin to experience ASL poetry as Deaf people do.

The following transcripts of Lerner's captions at performances of "Wise Old Corn #1" and "Ode to Words" fail to do these poems justice. In fact, the Flying Words Project does not consider what follows to be poetry at all. As Lerner explains, "If we were going to do written poems alone, we would have had more latitude in words to choose from." Even so, Cook and Lerner develop the English component with literary brio; for example, ribbons of an untitled Pablo Neruda poem are threaded through "Ode to Words." While the public awaits more translations to access the rich body of ASL poetry, the Flying Words Project is the nonsigner's best way to glimpse what this art has to offer. And that, as demonstrated by the Flying Words Project and the few translations available of other ASL poets, is a lot.

Flying Words Project was established in 1984 at the Rochester Institute of Technology when hearing poet Jim Cohn introduced Cook, then a Deaf graphic design major, to Lerner, a hearing visiting instructor in the history department. Cook had already been performing imaginative and cadenced storytelling in ASL, but Cohn suggested that he think about performing for the public beyond the signing community and praised Lerner as a brilliant interpreter. (Lerner would later say, "I don't understand why Jim said that; I have never worked as an interpreter before.") Their relationship soon became thoroughly collaborative; they developed sign pieces together before crafting "captions," not full translations but carefully placed information, for Lerner to voice while Cook signed onstage. In some fantastically complex pieces, a second pair of hands is needed, and Lerner joins Cook onstage.

Flying Words Project has become an institution, demonstrating the power of creative expression across languages and cultures. The duo has won many grants, including support from the Puffin Foundation, the New York State Council for the Arts, and the National Endowment for the Arts. Many publications have given Cook and Lerner special recognition and critics' choice awards, among them *Village Voice*, *Drama-logue*, and the Los Angeles and Chicago *Readers*. Flying Words Project has performed at Gallaudet, Harvard, Ohio State University, the 16th International Poetry Festival (Rotterdam, The Netherlands), Swarthmore, the University of California at San Diego, the Whitney Museum, and the Walker Institute of Art, as well as many other places across the United States, Canada, and Europe. A large selection of Flying Words Project pieces has been compiled into a videotape titled *The Can't Touch Tour*.

Wise Old Corn #1

This poem is about change. And we have several images we want to show you before it starts. You might remember from the Summer Olympics of 1968 that two Black Americans won first and second places and during the awards ceremony, they gave a Black Power salute, which is a very powerful image.

Another image is from the Native Americans. They would have a special dance called the Sun Dance. And what they would do is they would take a piece of wood, very sharp . . . pierce their chest with it, and tie a rope, and then hang from it. This was a very special spiritual experience.

This poem has magic seeds that can become anything. They can become a star or a building . . . a bridge, anything.

This poem is dedicated to Archbishop Romero, a lady poet named Carolyn Forché . . . wonderful woman, of course Martin Luther King, and to all people who plant seeds.

> He said, "I have a dream"
> that shattered
> shot
> earth
> earth
> shot right through
> the earth
> while a beating heart needs comforting.

This piece is called "Wise Old Corn #1."

> Planted
> Growing branches of understanding
> beauty
>
> A quarter moon shimmering on branches
> moon shine
> up the tree trunks

flowing
river
flowing
through a boulder gateway
and flowing to a reflection of the moon
the moon!

Reflection is split by a canoe
trees, trees
paint his face
paint his face
A low hanging branch over long braided hair
like a headdress of leaves (brushes by)

Wise old corn
tears off a leaf
a row of kernels
then he husks the whole corn
rows of kernels.

A yellow seed
the seed explodes into life.
The flower cup
its center
a swirling fugue
under the sun
and flower
reach to touch
as the blazing sun
brilliant sun
sleepy sun
he sets in the West
covering himself with a sparkling star blanket
stars and constellations
under a sky of infinite space.

The star studded sword of a Roman constellation
If you connect the dots . . .
They make his helmet
breastplates
metal skirt
and curved shield
sparkling.

Sheathes the sword and pulls out the moon
and its reflection.
A reflection that's split by a canoe.

This brown seed will become a star
flung up, up
it explodes in the sky
a brand new star.

A yellow seed flung up
exploding . . . a new star.

A black seed becomes olympic gold metal
star spangled
black powered salute
that explodes in the sky
a star.

A red seed flung.
It's a bare chest
skewered to a rope
and pulled, pulled into the sky
exploding, a star.

The Roman plucks out a solar eye
and then flings it
down

down
towards
the canoer's chest cavity expands with heat
The warmth flows from his heart up to his head.

This seed will build a bridge
from one bank to the other
a suspension bridge.

And then rising from the ground
growing
a church
steeple
bell
bell
doors
doors
open to a black congregation
by ones
twos
threes
and fours
singing hallelujah
and marching
with determination.

They face the river
the bridge
and they face the black boots
the tightened belt
fireman's hat and badge
fire hose
power lines powered on.
It's a water cannon!

But they march anyways.

Fireman, with a jet stream
he smashes his face.
I said, he smashes his face

Jet stream pounding
pounding
water forms
chains of water
that drain right off this black man.

Then the fireman blows away marchers
just blows them away
in a hurricane of rage
that chains him.

Jet stream
he turns toward another
and blasts him
shoes fly off
fire hose drags him down the street
smashed on a storefront

this raging stream of images
captured
on NBC
where it's transmitted up up
to a satellite
then down, down
To the antennae
of a house
into the wiring
to the television set
where you sit watching
as the fire hose drags him down the street
smashed into a storefront

This image
a shot of knowledge
that goes from your head
down
down
to your heart
a heart that needs comforting.

Ode to Words

It's a bible
It's a boat.
Blowing dust
on the waves
on the waves
at the shores
of the new world.

It's a palm tree fully laden
coconuts dropping down.

It's a Mayan temple
of engraved steps . . .
a snake of stone . . .
a macaw frozen in flight . . .
an eternal scream

And at the top
standing amongst
poles of flames reflect the Mayan king.
The king
in his ceremonial headdress.
he welcomes the Spaniard.

Then he summons off of the rock,
a Mayan sun
cheeks
lips
rays
hair and beard rays.

He gives life to plants
and they breathe together.

He summons forth
the birth
of a Mayan woman.
Breasts
belly
cervix.
She
gives
life.
And then returns to the womb.

He summons
a Mayan temple
with a king
and a crown
with a sword
in prayer
he gives blood.

The Spaniard
he turns the page
pulls out a sword.
Breaks it
Spins it.

It swirls into a funnel
a funnel of words
swirling
a hurricane
a hurricane that chases down the man
who screams as he is sucked up into the funnel.

Then the storm
hovers over a river.
Waters pulled
pulled
As the river winds up

into the storm
which disappears into the book.

And the Spaniard turns the page
and a word escapes.
Words flowing off the pages.
Words . . . a regiment of words
line a field of maize

Words march forward.
They devour the field.
Like locusts
they swarm the temple
crumbling
snake erodes
macaw disintegrates
and the man screams as he's eaten off the wall.

Palm trees
ground down
down
into dust.

With an empty book
in a boat fully laden,
he carries off the gold . . .
carries off the gold.

Leaving behind desolation
rubble
and a cross.

But
from beneath a broken rock is a glistening.
It's a word.
He tastes it.
shares it.

A word cracked is a rainbow.
Grammar when stretched out
forms a school of fish.
a bullfrog.

A word caught.
He peels it
and then grates it down into dust
and then breathes it in.

Sentences like spaghetti slurped up.
Punctuation points picked off like grapes.

Water
refreshing ASL!
The juices form a lake
and he licks it.

Questions
answers
sex
sweat . . .
It all goes into the broth.

It's a painter
and his canvas;
a forest of trees
a red tailed falcon
a butterfly

Poetree
leaves
falling
falling towards its reflection
in the river.

That's poetry
poetry
poetry
it's the bombay doors opening
the mushroom clouds
eating away hair
skin
teeth
bones
he's gone!

Words
words
and he carries off the gold
carries off the gold.

Katrina R. Miller (1965–) and Damara Goff Paris (1965–)

TWO DECADES AFTER the invention of the cochlear prosthesis in 1957, the artificial hearing device began to be implanted widely among deaf children. This sparked no small amount of controversy, as many Deaf people found it threatening. It became the target of outrage in a dizzying catalogue of works of art and literature, and Katrina R. Miller and Damara Goff Paris wrote one of the best pieces in response to not only the implant but also its perceived purpose: an audist denial of deafness. Miller, who is a hearing signer, and Paris, who is Deaf, each has a deaf sibling who underwent cochlear implantation, Miller's unsuccessfully. Paris states, "I support the right of adults to receive the implant. I have more concerns about children being implanted." The writers of "How the Audist Stole ASL" succeed spectacularly in commandeering Theodor "Dr. Seuss" Geisel's classic *How the Grinch Stole Christmas!*, which was first published in 1957, the same year the cochlear implant was invented. Miller says their adaptation demonstrates that, "like the spirit of Christmas, ASL cannot be suppressed."

Katrina R. Miller and Damara Goff Paris were both born in 1965. Miller was raised with a deaf sibling in Topeka, Kansas. She earned her bachelor's degree in sociology and women's studies from the University of Alaska in 1993 before studying rehabilitation counseling in deafness at Western Oregon University, where she got her master's degree. In 2001, Miller received her doctorate in Deaf studies and Deaf education from Lamar University, and a book based on her dissertation was published two years later as *Deaf Culture Behind Bars: Signs and Stories of a Texas Population*. She is associate professor at Emporia State University.

Paris was born and raised in the Bay Area of California. She became deaf and a right-leg amputee at the age of two after an accident. Paris also earned a master's degree in rehabilitation counseling in deafness from Western Oregon University. Of Cherokee and Blackfoot descent, she served for four years as president of the Intertribal Deaf Council. She has published six books, including *Step into the Circle: The Heartbeat of American Indian, Alaska Native and First Nations Deaf Communities*, and *The Highpoint of Persistence*.

How the Audist Stole ASL

Every Deafie
In the DEAF-WORLD
Liked ASL a lot . . .

But the Audist,
Who lived North of Gallaudet,
Most certainly did NOT!

The Audist hated ASL! The whole signing scene!
Please don't ask why. No one knows why he was so mean.
It could be that he did not understand language by eye.
It could be, perhaps, that his philosophy wasn't Bi-Bi.*
But I think that the most likely reason of all
May have been that his heart was two sizes too small.

But,
Whatever the reason,
His heart or his mind,
He stood there near campus, hating the signs,
Staring down from his clinic with a sour, angry frown
At the bright kitchen lights where they signed in their town.
For he knew every Deafie in the DEAF-WORLD beneath
Was busy now, planning their NAD retreat.

"They're having a Miss Deaf USA pageant," he sneered.
"Tomorrow's the convention! It's practically here!"
Then he made a promise most binding:
"I must find a way to keep those Deafies from signing!"
For, tomorrow, he knew . . .

---

* Bilingualism-Biculturalism (Bi-Bi) is an education movement supporting the natural and cultural use of American Sign Language along with written English for instructing deaf children.

All the Deafies in the DEAF-WORLD
Would start their manual talk
Not going around, but 'tween others they'd walk.
Tapping on shoulders and flicking the lights,
Hugging and visiting long into the night.

All the Deaf, young and old, would sit down for a chat.
And they'd sign! And they'd sign!
AND they'd SIGN! SIGN! SIGN! SIGN!
They'd chat about their schools and tell ABC stories
And the Audist found all this quite droll and boring.

And THEN,
They'd do something he liked least of all,
Every Deafie in the DEAF-WORLD, the tall and the small,
Would assemble together, with eyes open wide,
As onto their stage, Howie Seago would stride.*

They'd watch! And they'd watch!
AND they'd WATCH! WATCH! WATCH! WATCH!
And the more the Audist thought of their visual claps,
The more the Audist thought, "I must stop this manual yap!
Why, for more than 100 years I've put up with it now!
I MUST stop ASL from existing!
. . . But, HOW?"

Then he got an idea!
An awful idea!
THE AUDIST
GOT A HORRIBLE, AWFUL IDEA!

He fashioned a machine. The Audist was a believer
In that bionic device with its shiny receiver.†
He proclaimed it successful, painless, and quick,
"It will make you hearing, lickety-split!

---

* Howie Seago is an accomplished Deaf actor.
† In other words, the cochlear implant.

Katrina R. Miller and Damara Goff Paris   219

"All I need is a patient . . . "
The Audist looked all around.
But patients were scarce; there were none to be found.
Did that stop the Audist . . . ?
No! The Audist simply said,
"If I can't find a willing candidate, I'll convince parents instead!"
So he printed up pretty brochures with blue ink
To promote miracle surgery for Deaf offspring.

Their windows were dark. Snow filled the air.
All the Deafies were signing in their sleep without care
As he crept past Alice Cogswell out in the square.
"This is stop number one," the Audist hissed.
He crawled through a window, brochures in his fist.

Then he slithered and slunk, with a smile most contrary,
Into Stokoe's old basement, taking every ASL dictionary.
He took *Children of a Lesser God* and *SIGN ME ALICE* scripts,
And *Deaf Way* and *Silent News* just for kicks.*
And he shoved them in bags. Then the Audist, very grimly,
Stacked them to burn in the university chimney!

The Audist shoved the DPN exhibit in his sack
When a figure appeared in the library stacks.
He turned around fast and he saw a young Deafie!
It was little "C-to-the-shoulder," who was no more than three.

The Audist had been caught by this small Deafie daughter
Who'd crawled out of bed for a cup of cool water.
She stared at the Audist and in tiny signs, said, "Hey!
Why are you taking our culture away?"

---

    * *Children of a Lesser God* is an award-winning play by hearing playwright Mark Medoff that features Deaf characters; *SIGN ME ALICE* is a play by Deaf actor and writer Gil Eastman; *The Deaf Way* is a book about the first international cultural arts conference of the Deaf, held at Gallaudet University in 1989 under the directorship of Mervin D. Garretson; and *Silent News* was the leading Deaf newspaper from 1969 to 2002.

But, you know, that old Audist was so smart and so slick
He thought up a lie and he thought it up quick!
He smiled kindly, a benevolent mask.
"You should speak, yes indeed, you must 'pass.'
I only want the best for you, my dear,
To fix your ears proper so you can hear."

And his fib fooled the child. So he shaved her head
And sent her to surgery on a big hospital bed.
And when little "C-to-the-shoulder" fell asleep from the drug,
He picked up his scalpel and into her skull, he dug.

And then the very last thing that he pried
Was the mastoid bone from inside.
Then he slunk out the back alley door, the old liar.
In her ear he left nothing but electrodes and wire.

Then
He went into
The other Deafies' homes

Leaving brochures
And videos
And CI tomes

It was just past dawn at the Audist's clinic,
When he rushed into the office at the very last minute.
He placed an OPEN sign on the door,
Waiting for customers. Oh! How he'd $core!
So the Audist put his hand to his brow and he squinted
But no customers appeared, despite how he'd hinted.
So in puzzlement, onto the street he sprinted.

Staring down at Gally,
The Audist started howling.
They were all signing, the Deafies hadn't quit!
They were out on the green, quoting Veditz!*

Every Deafie in the DEAF-WORLD, the tall and the small,
Were signing! Without any voicing at all!
He HADN'T stopped ASL from existing!
It EXISTED!
Their chance to be hearing, they'd totally missed it!

And the Audist, scalpel in pocket,
Stood puzzling and puzzling, "How could they knock it?
They're signing with pride! They're signing with style!
They're using ASL in schools, restaurants, and grocery store aisles!"
He puzzled for hours, and then he puzzled some more.
And he puzzled until his puzzler was sore.
"Maybe it's not about English oration . . .
Maybe it's all about communication!"

And what happened then . . . ?
Well . . . in the DEAF-WORLD they say
That the Audist's small heart
Grew three sizes that day!
And the minute his heart didn't feel quite so tight,
He tossed away his scalpel with all of his might.
And he brought back the DPN exhibit!
And the classic Deaf Lit!
And he . . .

. . . HE HIMSELF . . . !
The Audist took an ASL class
And learn it, he did!

---

* George W. Veditz (1861–1937), twice the president of the National Association of the Deaf, called for the preservation of sign language in the face of spreading oralism. In a 1913 film, he signed an address in which he stated that "sign is the noblest gift God gave deaf man."

Raymond Luczak
(1965–)

FOR THOSE WHO WENT to public schools instead of schools for the Deaf, Raymond Luczak's poems are overwhelmingly familiar. It is surreal how many of their experiences are the same, down to the smallest details and to each emotional wound inflicted by all manner of neglect and rejection. His long journey from being a walking island to his discovery of the Deaf world and self-awakening is also shared by many. Along the way, there are many pitfalls, setbacks, and wrong turns.

Almost all deaf people get their first taste of the medical perspective of deafness at the audiologist's office, and the message that something is wrong with them is immediate. Even though the audiologist is a rare personification of audism—most forms of audism are impossibly subtle—the medical professional in "The Audiologist" remains vague. Thus, the audiologist serves as a living metaphor for the difficulty in pointing out the foe, making the Deaf child's "war" as much against himself as anyone else.

The unaccommodating teacher and cruel hearing peers of "Spelling Bee 1978" are also the enemies, yet the Deaf boy is riddled with self-doubt and longing and is unable to assert himself without feeling shame. But then he glimpses a better future, a better self, when he learns how to sign in "Learning to Speak, Part I." This poem displays Luczak's artistic cunning in modifying the Sapphic stanza form with a dash of awkwardness, almost as if he is learning how to write the poem just as the narrator is learning a new language. After learning it, the boy in "Hummingbirds" "sat up and freed / [his] deaf voice" in the presence of hearing classmates. But when they mock him, he stops short. He needs more cultural grounding, and where better to start than with Laurent Clerc? When Clerc takes the place of Christ in the fantasy realm of "The Crucifixion," Luczak explores how the act of embracing Deaf culture resembles a religious conversion. Finally, the adult Luczak knows who he is as a Deaf person well enough to write, in "Instructions to Hearing Persons Desiring a Deaf Man," not only a self-portrait but also a manual for how others should treat and understand him.

Raymond Luczak was born in Michigan and presumably became deaf when he was seven months old due to double pneumonia. He attended oral programs for deaf children but learned the manual alphabet in secret in 1979. A year later, he was allowed to learn Signing Exact English. Luczak did not learn American Sign Language until he decided to enter Gallaudet University in 1984, instead of a local technical college. In 1988, he graduated magna cum laude with a degree in English. Then Luczak moved to New York City and worked for a dozen years in computer technology support until becoming a full-time writer. His books include *St. Michael's Fall: Poems, Silence Is a Four-Letter Word: On Art & Deafness, This Way to the Acorns: Poems, Snooty: A Comedy*, and the novel *Men with Their Hands*, which won a prestigious award for gay fiction. More than a dozen of his plays have been produced, and some of them are collected in *Playing It by Eye*. He is also an accomplished filmmaker.

The Audiologist

The thick gray windows never reveal
her shadowy figure. The audiologist
always has something to conceal
behind those windows. She only reveals
to Mom how I did this year. I steal
a look at my audiogram and her checklist.
The thick gray windows never reveal
her shadowy figure: The audiologist

and I are at war
over my ears, my headphones, my chair.
First she makes a beep, or a low roar—
and then I'm at war
with myself. Did I truly hear
that or not? My hand shoots up in the air,
volleying against her score
over my ears, my headphones, my chair.

The thick walls absorb my silence.
I cannot hear anything from outside,
except through my ear-burning, tense
headphones. They absorb her silence.
I wrestle with my ears, my conscience,
as I close my eyes to listen, decide.
The thick walls absorb my silence
as her sounds come from the other side.

Spelling Bee 1978

A giddiness overtook my entire
soul when Jeanine misspelled. I knew
the word: T-I-M-B-U-K-T-U.
My ears, my eyes were taut as a wire,
zipping between Sister Priscilla and
my class for clues to the next word on her
lips . . . I'd given up TV night after
night, looking up words I didn't understand
and memorizing them. I had to hide
away, I imagined how they would sound,
so in the basement I spoke them out loud
and prayed they'd pronounce the same way as I . . .
The day had come: Now Jeanine shook her head
and groaned as I turned happy in my dread.

Michelle, Lee Ann and I stood near the door
while everyone watched the teacher's pencil
check off words already used. She was still
on the second list, I knew not much more
was left: She'd followed more or less what I'd
remembered from my lists. But sometimes she'd
abruptly pick from a different list: Feed-
back squealed from my hearing aids when I'd
tried to hear her better. That was what
I dreamed most, those looks as if I should
have been *prepared*, she'd done all she could
to help me understand the word. "What?"
Her face tightened: No, I didn't deserve
those privileged repeats. I hated her nerve.

As I watched Michelle, and then Lee Ann, spell
their words correctly, I thought of The Friend
sitting behind Greg's desk. Among the "friends"

in my class, he'd given me the most hell:
He laughed when he saw how I couldn't play
with a dog-chewed green Nerf football. He knew
I'd wanted friends but he never cared to
say hello. I hoped. But he looked away,
slapped fives with his new friends, and nudged Tony
and Greg at me. I stood under the eaves
as I stared at the puddles filled with brown leaves.
I imagined bumps of potholes only
tiny islands expecting coconut
trees and warm winds. There was always a *but* . . .
I discovered, when I turned off my aids
and watched The Friend assert basketball rules,
I felt less lonely in not having to
hear everything, in sharp relief, that made
a playground. Standing by myself, I dreamed
of being buddies with The Friend. We'd ride
our bikes all over Ironwood; he'd cry
out whoops as he dared to drop low and lean,
now slowing down around corners downtown.
We'd snicker with a look when old ladies
jumped back to let us by. We'd see movies
and lurk together in alleys downtown.
That nothingness in my hearing aids was
sweeter in somehow softening his loss.

Now in the classroom, he made ugly faces.
I ignored him as Sister Priscilla
gave me another glance—that Attila
the Hun look—as she repeated the name.
"What?" I racked my brains—what did it sound most
like? I mouthed to myself the word, not sure
what I was saying. The Friend looked assured,
his not-again glances striking the coast
of faces looking back at me. Would I
make it? "It's a thing?" "—Yes." "Where is it in?"
"—You know the rules." Pages of the list in

my head stayed picture-perfect in my eyes.
"How many syllables?" She repeated as
I sought for clues in the eyes of my class.

They revealed nothing, but I counted three
syllables: Where was it in my memory?
"Sa . . . lack . . . tight?" "We don't have any
more time." She didn't move, she looked at me.
"I don't know . . . S-A- . . . L-A-C-K-T-
I-T-E?" "Close!" I watched her on the board:
STALACTITE. I thought how Mom had explored
those dark caverns once, before she had me:
"Why didn't you say Kentucky?" My ears
burned when I realized I'd just talked back to
Sister Priscilla! Her face turned hard. "—You
sit down, and we'll all finish up here."
I did so while The Friend tugged at his ears
for me. I bled quietly in laughter's fear.

Learning to Speak, Part I

Mary Hoffman, didn't you know what you had
done when you drove all the way from Ramsay, those
photocopies sitting beside you in
your car?
       Your long blonde
hair, thin fingers, a tiny waist and eyes that
lit up at how I'd imitated signs off
your hands as we turned over the page for the
next sign, an arrow
indicating how I should whoosh right through the
air, my palms flat like airplane wings and yet so
coordinated with my mind, buffeted by
    seeing Ironwood's
    only deaf man, Gramps.

                         He worked evenings at
Hurley's Holiday Inn, in its kitchen where
he was dishwasher. Afternoons he sat in
    front of the bar near
Santini's Gift Shoppe, his hands folded on
lap until one kid or two came with their hands
fingerspelling their names or something until
    he smiled, or laughed. He
would then fingerspell, slowly, so that they could
understand it. I stared at his lips, hardly
moving.

      I thought how I hated my voice, the
      faces everyone
      in my class made when I tried to explain what
      I had meant: Why couldn't I just sit there like
      him, not having to say anything? I sneaked
      into the public

library and found some old sign language books.
I took them home, hiding them in my Jacquart's
burlap bookbag and reading them upstairs where
no one would catch me
trying arrows, wriggles and stillness on the
bed. Sometimes I'd hear quite suddenly the click
of the downstairs door opening—I'd slam my
book shut and cover
it with something else so no one would ever
think I was learning to be Gramps in secret.

And I rather liked the blue Deaf-Mute Cards he'd passed
out. One found its way
home: our kitchen table. I picked it up, piqued:
Who was that man, smiling with ears sticking out?
"My name . . . GRAMPS, a Deaf-Mute . . . Thank you so
     much for
your kindness." Handshapes
showed how A to Z could be formed; I wondered
how this contraband piece was smuggled in, and
left just so with Mom kneading dough right next to
it. I stared, thinking:

> Does it mean I'm allowed to learn? I learned it
> anyway. The handshapes fit so easily,
> naturally. It got so I practiced running
> through everyone I
> knew until their names felt natural on my
> fingers.

>   Late at night I dreamed of a voiceless
> world, where everyone signed and understood me.
> Lipreading would be
> banished, or at least, expectations of me
> having to lipread. I longed to be more deaf,
> mute like Gramps who sat in front of Hulstrom's and

waved when I sped by
on my ten-speed bicycle.

                              I wanted to
stop, to see his eyes take me in with my
earmolds sticking out like his ears too under
his baseball cap. I
wanted not to have to say anything, to
isolate myself from the rest of them, the
boys who laughed at my nasal speech, Father
K's silent gazes,
and the teachers' apologetic looks. Well,
if I couldn't hear as well as they, I thought:
Might as well learn.

                        So Mom told me then, that
you would come in our
house to teach me what you knew. They seemed resigned,
as if they'd expected I'd learn it anyway.
You came frequently, and then you called Mom to
apologize, I
can't come today. She told me later you had
multiple sclerosis. I couldn't see you
in my mind: your fingers frozen, unable to
lift?

    The next time you
came, you only said, Sorry, I was sick, and
opened to where we'd stopped the last time. Then
came the day I *knew*, that I wouldn't see you
again, not for a
long time.

        Later I took to riding into
town and seeking Gramps on his bench. I parked my
bike beside where he sat, and talked for some time.

We fingerspelled to
each other as passersby shook their heads at
us, deaf people: Look how they can talk without
voices!

Mary Hoffman, didn't you know what
you had begun when
you agreed to teach me my first, and then, the
next sign until I couldn't stop, not until
I became Gramps, not mute but raging instead,
hands howling volumes?

Hummingbirds

Our new Sheet Metal teacher left
us boys alone in the cafeteria.

    My notebook was filled
    with sugarcubes of want

One of them said, "Hey you!
What you doin' over there?"

    My fingers were only
    hummingbirds in a small cage

I sat up and freed
my deaf voice, my hearing hands

    They fluttered under my chin,
    in front of my chest, everywhere

The boys' eyes narrowed like a cat's
for a minute. Then they stood up.

    My voice faltered as I felt
    their fierce wings beating

"Fairy! Look at his hands
swishing in the air!"

    Lilacs' fragrances melted
    under globs of solder

The boys flaunted limp wrists.
I shot all my birds in mid-flight.

The Crucifixion

I was only an innocent boy at the time.
My parents tried to explain to me
what the word "crucifixion" meant,
but I could not lipread them.
As I trailed after them for Jerusalem,
they chatted amiably with each other,
and met a caravan of speech
therapists who chatted amiably too.
They frowned on every gesture I made
when I tried to speak more clearly.
My voice was not good enough. I turned
my hearing aids, but all I heard was
their seamless chatter.

Ravens leaped from their olive trees,
wings spreading wide for the winds.
They were also coming to Jerusalem.
My parents always covered their ears
when they let out a series of caw-caws.
I loved them because they were so loud.
And their wings! They were a joy to watch,
their chest-beating show of power.
Some distance behind us there were people
laughing and pointing at the ravens.
They did not talk, but their bodies sang
with their hands: the most beautiful caw-caw.

My parents saw them too, and promptly turned me
around to the front. I imagined
speech therapists whispering to them:
He must learn to speak right. I practiced

my *st*'s, *r*'s, and *w*'s with fervor.
They clapped hands whenever I got them right.
You're saved from those barbarian hands.
My parents' eyes had never been so full of relief
they almost cried. Over the last hill before
Jerusalem, I saw the smooth mound of Calvary Hill
rise high. While my parents pointed at it,
I stole a glance back at those weird people.
They must be gypsies, I thought. There,
an older man winked at me, his gnarly hands
gesturing I should throw away my hearing aids.
I riveted my eyes back to the road.
My father tousled my hair,
for I now knew better than to stare;
he'd said gypsies always kidnapped children
like me, and they never saw their parents again.

As I scampered down the dusty road, I tripped
and knocked a boy down. Our hearing aids clashed
like jolts of volts: We got up and looked
at each other. I pointed to his hearing aid,
wondering why he had one when I had two.
He pointed to his empty ear and shook his head.
He turned abruptly still when our parents stood
behind us. I looked up at the angry faces
of our speech therapists. My mother compared notes
with my friend's mother while we hungered
after each other's hands. Finally—and
suddenly—my father said, "We mustn't be late."
We hurried on, before the gypsies could come
close. They became quiet when they recognized
our speech therapists surrounding
the two of us. I gave them a smile:
Their hands flurried suddenly into wings.
We doubled our pace, and so gained quick

admission into the city. I looked behind
and saw the gates closing on them.
My friend and I looked at each other, suddenly lost.

Huge ravens alighted on the eaves of roofs
and clotheslines buoying on the wind. My caravan
melted into the crowd's clamor for the death
of Laurent Clerc, the gypsy who'd claimed to be
the king of us all. As we pushed our way closer,
the road became covered with broken shrapnel pieces
of hearing aids. They smoked like burnt cinders.
My parents didn't even notice, they were too busy
chanting. I looked around and caught a woman
whose mouthing didn't fit in with the crowd's chants.
Then I saw there were many of *them*, mouthing
without a sound. My friend's eyes also blinked:
There were gypsies right in our midst!

The crowd's electricity changed when the Roman
soldiers shoved to clear the way for Clerc.
I bent low and followed my friend to the forefront
where we could see him better. There he was:
dragging along a cross made of piano boards.
Sweat dripped from his chubby body,
soaking his loincloth of a hearing aid harness.
His double chin sagged from awkward speech,
his throat swelled from a thousand therapists' hands,
his naked feet bled from the sharp metallic cinders.
Right behind his heels was King Alexander Graham Bell.[*]
I quaked in his stern presence, his long gray beard
flapping in the wind. Ravens stretched their claws
back and forth while they circled above him.
I watched King Bell flay Clerc's crisscrossed back
with a whip of piano strings, and saw his eyes glow

---

[*] Bell (1847–1922), the inventor of the telephone, championed oralism and eugenics. He also cautioned against the creation of a "deaf variety of the human race."

when he saw how Clerc couldn't speak. His hands
were wild with rage, trying to let go his cross.
I saw a thousand tears in the eyes of disguised gypsies.
King Bell whipped him again, and again,
proclaiming, "You must speak! You must speak!"
The crowds picked up on this, chanting along.
Clerc fell at last, his face now ruptured by the sharp
edges of broken hearing aids. I broke out of
the crowd and pulled the cross off his back.
Clerc's eyes spoke with tender thanks
as King Bell stared at my hearing aid harness.

"How dare you do this to him? He doesn't deserve
your pity." I tried to answer,
but the words came out all wrong. He drummed
his fingers on his elbow as I tried again,
and again. He smiled whenever I got a word
right, and said, "Good. Say it again, but remember
to make your *t*'s clearer." The crowd turned
enormously silent as I spoke slowly:
"You . . . don't . . . have . . . to . . . hurt . . . people."
They clapped furiously while King Bell hugged me
and shouted, "See? He speaks so well!
This boy will be my heir." He tousled my hair
as he beckoned me to step aside. I watched him
brandish his whip before Clerc twitched again.
Bits of hearing aids dug into his flesh.
King Bell kicked his sides until Clerc turned over.
He bent down and said slowly into his face,
"Do you understand what this boy said? He said,
'You don't have to hurt people.' That's a lot
more intelligent than you could say with hands!"

Clerc took a deep sigh and heaved himself up.
His eyes locked on mine as he mouthed slowly
so I could lipread. His gestures said:
You like talk? Your-hands easy—

King Bell whupped his hands short.
"I understood every sign you made!" *
The crowd turned to watch his queen Mabel's hands fly:†
It's true, he's right—"No." He looked
around, and signed very bluntly something.
It looked like a whip. Her face dropped, grim.
King Bell ordered his soldiers to lift the cross
back on Clerc's shoulders. As I watched the two
dissolve into the following crowds on Calvary Hill,
I felt a man's hand stroke my shoulders softly.
He had to be one of them. I followed him
through a maze of alleys to a tiny room upstairs.
The windows were covered with burlap curtains
as he lit a candle. The room burst into gypsies
surrounding my friend, who had no harness on.
He was the happiest boy I had ever seen.
They imitated animals and all sorts of people,
and he laughed. I couldn't help it either,
and found our fingers groping for their signs.

Later that day we stole our way towards Calvary Hill.
Alice Cogswell's face looked sad as she prayed
nearby until she recognized one of us. Her face
lit up with unspeakable joy as she looked around
to make sure no one was watching our hands
flickering near our waists, away from our faces.
Babies future same again never. Proud my s-o-n.
We nodded, not looking directly into Clerc's face
while his flabby arms sagged on the cross. We tried
not to feel the rusty nails staked in the heart
of his hands. Say last words couldn't. I looked
into her eyes, hardly silenced with rage.
I watched the bored gazes of King Bell's guards

---

* Bell's devotion to oralism did not stop him from becoming a fluent signer and preaching directly to Deaf people.

† Mabel Hubbard Bell (1857–1923), deaf since age five, studied speech under Alexander Graham Bell and later became his wife.

before I said, I-f he-can't, many-many future-will say
last words his. The gypsies tried not to appear
too excited as they led me out of the city. Ravens
swooped playfully all over us, caw-cawing noisily.
As I walked past the front steps of the king's temple,
I noticed the frantic footsteps of speech therapists
paid to convince parents teaching Speech was the Way,
the Only Way into the larger world. After I'd left
Jerusalem, I looked back on Calvary Hill.
Clerc's cross was no longer a shadow looming starkly
in the evening sun. Instead outstretched hands reached
higher into the sky, and they were all our own.

Instructions to Hearing Persons
Desiring a Deaf Man

His eyebrows cast shadows everywhere.
You are a difficult language to speak.

His long beard is thick with distrust.
You are another curiosity seeker.

His hands are not cheap trinkets.
Entire lives have been wasted on you.

His face is an inscrutable promise.
You are nothing but paper and ink.

His body is more than a secret language.
Tourists are rarely fluent in it.

His eyes will flicker with a bright fire
when you purge your passport of sound.

Let your hands be your new passport,
for he will then stamp it with approval.

A deaf man is always a foreign country.
He remains forever a language to learn.

Abiola Haroun
(1970–)

WHILE ABIOLA HAROUN did attend Gallaudet and, afterward, kept her connection to the signing community, she was never exposed to the writings of other Deaf poets—that is, until she fell in love with Loy E. Golladay's collection of poetry in a public library. This discovery led her to take her passion for writing to a higher level by enrolling in a master of fine arts program in creative writing. What is interesting about her three poems here is that all of them were written before she read Golladay's work. That they share the same themes, and even the same imagery, with much of Deaf poetry is a testament to how similar the Deaf experience can be for very different people. Though she says nothing new in her praise of signing over speech, the suffering of Deaf people, the saving grace of deafness, or the beauty of "eye music," Haroun's poems have their own voices, each with their individual charm, that add much to the canon. She manages to avoid the pitfalls of many other Deaf poets who write unwittingly—until or if they finally come across the work of other Deaf poets—what are mere repetitions of what has already been written. It is also much to her credit that she did not write only as a Deaf person but also as a Black Deaf person, through "The Deaf Negro" imagining a history and claiming it as her own.

Abiola Haroun was born in Nigeria. She became deaf at age ten after a bout with chicken pox. Haroun moved to England as a child and attended Mary Hare Grammar School in Newbury, Berkshire. At seventeen, she moved to the United States to attend Gallaudet University, where she received her bachelor's degree in biochemistry and biology in 1994. She has worked as a chemist for the Washington Suburban Sanitary Commission, Baxter Inc., and Human Genome Sciences. Now an American citizen, Haroun lives in Maryland with her son, Matthew.

Deaf Mind

Think hear
see hearse
See speech
feel sad
Must talk
think lack
See sign
me smile

The Deaf Negro

Like t'aint enuf, they would mutter,
That he was born with bronzed skin
But was born into deeply dense silence too
And hears none the good Mahsah's whip
As it sang long lasting notes on his back
Under the heat of the sun, in whitely spotted fields.

It may be a curse in the minstrel's eye
That he felt none, the evil muttered at him—
Words which made even the boldest men cry,
Only they saw no manner of how
What a sheltered blessing it was truly
That no sinful words dared touch his silent soul.

While sitting in the green leafy fields
Tucked beside his noisy fellows,
He stares in thought and peacefully dreams,
Watching his hushed spirit flee
Into a world where freedom lies
Where none other yet, is set.

Ode to a Silent World

To a world wherein the days
Dwell as silent as nights
Where voiceless birds hum
Aloft in mute giant trees . . .

In which the mighty ocean roars
As quiet as tiny drops of rain
And the great wind blows across thy face
Stifled as a whispered voice

Where peace endures
In both my state of awakening and sleep
With thee as close to death as heaven to earth
And silent thunderstorms
Loud as Gibraltar crumbling
Awaken thee not

Where tiny footsteps and giant feet
Are confused odds of silent vibrations
Each sounding in harmony
As east turned into west

And fingers speak while hands sing
Echoing melodies of invisible drums
With tranquil mouths in motion
Uttering words lost into eternity.

Christopher Jon Heuer
(1970–)

THE SIX POEMS HERE by Christopher Jon Heuer make up three pairs: pangs of wistfulness, snapshots of a Deaf man under duress, and sarcastic scoffs. As different as these poems are, they all have Heuer's trademark intensity. "Visible Scars" is particularly illuminating about the difficulty in putting a finger to audism, which is most often subtle but very destructive, and the challenge of proving to people outside and inside the community that it does exist. The scars of audism are invisible, so Heuer pines for hearing slave overseers with whips to inflict visible scars. This is just one reason why Deaf poetry can be such a valuable political weapon. Heuer's poems succeed in making legible the scars created by a fellow deaf person in denial, a father who never signs, the charade of being "fine" among hearing nonsigners, and the dismissiveness of others, even those who know what it is like to be oppressed but whose scars are different. Both "Koko Want," which pokes fun at anthropologists' fascination with signing monkeys, and "We Can Save the Deaf!," a "fight song" of professionals in the "field of deafness," use satire to heal the wounds inflicted by their subjects.

Christopher Jon Heuer began to lose his hearing immediately after birth. He was fitted with his first hearing aid in the second grade and did not learn American Sign Language (ASL) until he was fourteen. Heuer attended public schools, except for two years at the Wisconsin School for the Deaf. He earned his bachelor's and master's degrees in English from the University of Wisconsin at Milwaukee. Heuer has worked in California, at various odd jobs, and with deaf students in the Milwaukee public schools. He met his wife, an ASL interpreter, while working as a camp counselor. In 1999, they moved to Virginia, and Heuer began teaching English at Gallaudet University. He has completed the coursework toward his doctorate in adult literacy and educational counseling from George Mason University, and is now working on his dissertation. Heuer has contributed to the anthologies *No Walls of Stone* and *The Deaf Way II Anthology*, and his collection of poetry is *All Your Parts Intact* (2003). In 2007, his social commentary was collected in *Bug: Deaf Identity and Internal Revolution*.

Bone Bird

You were a bird of bone.
Your wings held everything in
like a rib cage.
You said that deafness
was nothing, and took your
feathers from the dirt.
You blended in like a leaf
to its bed on a forest floor,
brother.

I said deafness was everything,
our blood and our flesh,
the air we breathed and flew in,
the kill in our talons.
I said that deafness was a song
to be spread out in a plume,
painted across the sky
like a rainbow. But to you

deafness was not a song.
With your tongue and your
bone beak and your rib-cage
wings, you blocked out more sky
than a scarecrow in a cornfield.
I painted your name in the air
but you looked away. You were
afraid of the sky, of your own
wings. You held everything in.

The Hands of My Father

Not once did my father sign to me.
He was a farmer; his explanations
were for the ground. Corn, rain,
earth—this was language,
the planting and bringing forth
of things. He did not like talking
to people, their noise and pace
and frantic lives. To him a sense

of hearing was only good for wind
and thunder, for the moaning
of cattle. I remember the hands
of my father, fingers clenched white
like teeth around the steering
wheels of tractors and the grips of
pitchforks; taking refuge from
the movement of my language

among the motions of his life.
Mine was not the kind of silence
that he knew, standing in rows
to be entered like a church—
undisturbed beyond the brush of
the leaves against his face and arms—
in the fields we would not cross
to meet one another.

My kind of silence was flood
and drought. He watched me
as if God had set the locusts on him.
His hands struck the dinner table
with the fast crack of lightning.

My silence was famine and disease,
forces of nature he could not
root out, or control. Or cure.

But now that he is dead, I see
his fingers in the corn, reaching
over the hills and fences to his son,
to say that he is sorry. At the
field's edge, the touch of each
kernel against my palm is a kiss
from his lips. I would go to him
if I knew where to walk.

Visible Scars

In my dream the old black woman
said *My but ain't you an uppity nigger*
for a white boy,
and threw a copy of the Americans with
Disabilities Act at my chest.

She said *What whip were you ever under?*
What land did you ever lose?
Then she showed me her back, tugging down
the heavy brown sweater that protected
her oppression. Her scars were black

in the way that skin visibly shudders
when ripped open, black in the way
that melanin reasserts itself in fury.
I reached for my ears but could not pull them off.
I felt in my ears but nothing was there.

I wished for scars like hers.
I wished to stand up and scream *Look!*
Look, look, look!
I wanted proof to show her, I wanted
centuries of songs to the Lord. I wished

for a hearing overseer
with a whip, I wished for rows of deaf men
in the cotton fields, singing in the sun.
I wished for the hearing man you could see,
so that I could point and shout

Look, look, look!
She said *Don't bring your anger here to me,*
white boy, and pointed at the door.
I left the interview with a deaf man's guilt,
because I had no proof.

Diving Bell

I am alone among familiar faces—
shiny fish that smile at me in hallways
and at dinners, blowing out their lists of
safe questions, sure to be understood. *How
are you*, sprayed out in a fury of white foam.
They wave their great fins so that I will know
it is me they are talking about. My
diving bell is heavy, the oxygen
turns bad fast. Nonetheless I say *I'm fine*.

How are you? Teeth flash and their eyes crinkle,
like happy piranhas. Blowing bubbles.
I laugh with them like I step on the brakes
of my car at red lights. Dull depths, gray streets.
Swimming through one intersection after
another, somewhere else to somewhere else.
On and off, words blinking Morse, or Chinese.
I choke in the bell, I kick myself dead.
The fish watch, and say that I am angry.

But that weight, all that weight. The pressure
builds, creating flying splinters that draw
blood. Going down. I say *I am fine*. Traffic
flows smooth around me, blinking on and off.
My hands are flat, white, pushing on the glass,
without gesture. There's no air, there's no air!
The fish follow me down in slow spirals,
nervous and a mystery. Somewhere else
to somewhere else. Nothing at all is wrong.

Koko Want[*]

(points) Koko want Super Meal #2.
You want what?
(points) Koko want Super Meal #2.
. . . you want . . . what?

The anthropologist is then consulted.
Give him a paper and pen.
Are you sure?
How should I know? The fries are on!
Fine, fine. Screw it. Here.

(writes) Koko want Super Meal #2.
I can't read his writing, man!
(points) Koko want Super Meal #2.
. . . I don't understand what he's saying!

Up comes the fry cook.
Can I help you?
(taps napkin) Koko want Super Meal #2.
You want a cheeseburger?
(shakes head) Koko want Super Meal #2.

You want fries?
(writes) Super Meal #2.
I don't understand.
(holds up napkin with #2 on it)

Koko want Super Meal #2.
You want Super Meal Number Two?

---

* Koko is a female lowland gorilla, born in 1971, who began to learn signs at age one. Koko, in the course of a study led by Dr. Francine Patterson, has acquired a working vocabulary of more than one thousand signs, the most advanced development in language that any nonhuman creature has achieved.

Nod of noble primate.
Extra large drink with that?
Nod of noble primate.

Thank you!
Fry cooks can always sign 'thank you.'
Something learned
from every cultural interaction.

We Can Save the Deaf!
(The Official Fight Song of Educators of the Deaf!)

Their voices are a screech on a broken treble clef!
Assign some singing therapy to close up all the rifts!
Raising up my hand; piano to my left!
Tap my tongue, click my teeth,
and we can save the Deaf! (Clap!)

It's almost sexual, rub their little throats!
Add some clouds and shrubbery;
they bleat like mountain goats!
Touch their forming mandibles! Chins a tiny cleft!
Teach them signs for "ball" and "tree"
and we can save the Deaf! (Clap!)

Put on plays! Work the script for days!
Let them run the printing press
and see how much it pays!
Brush their hair with hearing aids! We're daring
and we're deft!
Teach them to communicate
and we can save the Deaf! (Clap!)

Build them institutions! Sweeping dedications!
Teach them yes to nouns and verbs
and no to masturbation!
A tiny tummy tickle gives their lips a little lift!
Cochlear implant surgery—
and we can save the Deaf! (Clap!)

Their voices are a warble when they aren't at their best!
But strap them on a table, and we'll install the rest!
A few more statistics, and studies with a twist!
The more we know, the more we go
and we can save the Deaf! (Clap!)

Christopher Jon Heuer   255

Kristi Merriweather
(1971–)

WRITING HER POEMS IN Ebonics style—about being excited by an attractive, fellow Black Deaf person of the opposite sex and her rejection of any cultural labels other than her own for herself—Kristi Merriweather clearly performs one important social function of poetry. Poetry can be a gateway for one community to understand another. Through her language, hearing Blacks will find something familiar about her tone and some of her references and, therefore, will find it easier to appreciate what she is saying about also being Deaf. Non-Black Deaf readers can relate to Merriweather's happy surprise at finding, in the small signing community, a possible love interest who is like her. Readers can also relate to her independent spirit when it comes to labels and, at the same time, be introduced to what may be foreign to them. More broadly, this anthology serves the same function on many levels, especially by introducing the mainstream poetry-reading public to the Deaf world while aiming to increase the appreciation among Deaf people of poetry as a fine historical record and an art form.

Kristi Merriweather was born in Augusta, Georgia, and became deaf when she was two-and-a-half years old. A product of mainstreaming at public schools, she holds a bachelor's degree in psychology from Spelman College, a master's degree in psychology from Howard University, and a second master's degree in Deaf education from Georgia State University. Merriweather lives in College Park, Georgia, and is currently a teacher at the Atlanta Area School for the Deaf.

It Was His Movin' Hands

Know what I mean,
Don't you just know that feeling of
that thing white folks call
electricity sparking
that thing black folks like us call
good vibes
that gets that funky eyeplay started
our smiles manifesting,
rebelling
against our wishes
to appear
kool,
breezy kind of c-oo-ool, superfly
yeah, like that,
magick kickin' in,
sirens a-blarin'
peripheral vision gone malfunctioning
shoot,
it's obvious
we're losin' the control game,
shamelessly,
breakin' the rules,
ah, but
what's deafsista like me
gonna do, gonna do
with her mind shootin' up
into Milky Way, outta my reach,
when that fine brotha that we heard to be
with all that that we
ladies
call all that,
dang,
done the crime of visiblin' his presence to my eyes,

on the path to me,
nearer,
had the nerve to even pick up his chiseled hands
shapin' them, so familiar,
Hey, what was that, girl, did I see right?
lord, he be signin',
gonna be saying Hail Marys, Ebonic style,
if he be of non-hearing species
Ain't nothing else gettin' me
that 100 volts of good vibes
like a M.I.A.
finally returning to the land
out of fantasyisland,
Don't be botherin' me now,
I busy workin' it,
Magick in full effect now.

Be Tellin' Me

People tell me
what they think
a black deaf female is
People tell me
what they think
they know
what a black deaf female is
People tell me
they know the deal
behind all deals
just a simple solution
mix in the deaf culture,
add an equal amount of
black culture,
stir until smooth,
pronto, the black deaf culture,
I say
excuse my standard English, but
_____ you
I don't take no
second-handed,
mulatto,
prescribed,
whittled-down,
semi-that,
half-here,
part-this
culture,
uh-huh,
I be cookin' up my own recipe,
spicy, like mama taught me,
no, don't need your bowl,

thank you very much,
only I be
tellin' me
what a blakdeafemale is.

Pamela Wright-Meinhardt
(1971–)

"SILENT HOWL" AND "When They Tell Me . . . " together make a thorough prosecution of audism. The first represents an accomplishment that victims of oppression must attain before they can respond: to see through "the mask of benevolence." Pamela Wright-Meinhardt is not shy of doing this seeing subjectively, of mingling her protest with her observations. Some readers may find this poem, inspired by Allen Ginsberg's infamous poem, difficult to read, but it is indeed a howl—a barreling litany of the dizzying forms audism can, and does, take—and not meant for pleasant reading. In "When They Tell Me," written on Shakespeare's birthday, Wright-Meinhardt also delivers a familiar testimony of how those who speak up are often labeled everything but a decent human being.

Pamela Wright-Meinhardt was born in Birmingham, Alabama, and became deaf at the age of two after contracting spinal meningitis. She mostly attended public schools until she was fifteen, when she entered the Florida School for the Deaf and Blind, from which she graduated in 1988. Wright-Meinhardt then earned two bachelor's degrees from Gallaudet, in theater and English, and another pair of bachelor's degrees from the University of Great Falls (Montana), in secondary education and art. She taught at the Arizona School for the Deaf and Blind before joining the staff of *SIGNews*, a leading newspaper in the signing community. In 2006, she and her family moved to Minnesota; she and her husband, Matt, both now teach at the Minnesota State Academy for the Deaf. Wright-Meinhardt's work has appeared in many places, including *The Deaf Way II Anthology*, the original *Audism Monologues*, and on a T-shirt produced by the University of Wisconsin.

Silent Howl

I have seen the best souls of my world sodomized by a scheming uniform system and left to struggle, vegetating, for a breath of life.

I have seen intense camaradaries distorted and suppressed by a narrow, one-way, uncompromising larder of a society; determined cohesions crammed into incredible parodies and puppeteeringly masqueraded.

I have seen multitudes of children left alone in classrooms, misplaced and ignored, moved through grades and coddled, spoonfed, then kicked out into the cesspool of an incomprehensible reality tyrannically totalitarianed by those who can hear, and

I have seen the same darkness follow the same children home to loneliness and television, television, television, eating dinner in a closed little sphere and disappearing into bed unnoticed because Mommy and Daddy are too disinterested to try.

I have seen my language annihilated, mocked, shunned, belittled, doubted, analyzed, scientified, and butchered by know-it-alls who arrogantly believe their robotic hands emulate the natural unconscious grace of those who've internalized its fluency.

I have seen the beauty that flows from my hands researched, and researched, proved again and again to be valid then shoved into a clinical paragraph and skeptically disputed for scores of years.

I have seen pride hooked onto machines, machinated and cyborgic, programmed to repeatedly utter sounds difficult to decipher and shoved into grotesquely embarrassing, undignified positions; all for an experiment on his voice.

I have seen Kleenex, wooden tongue depressors, mirrors and fingers become tools of torture and writhing shame as condescending speech pathologists quote obscure success stories and wield a godly fist over unsuspecting and trusting frightened kids crunching themselves into the creases of their chairs.

I have seen children being told for years that their speech was ideal and beautiful then publicly humiliated by giggling perplexed teenagers ringing up the cash registers.

I have seen babies born into excited acceptance, proudly cherished and adulated in a world where voice finds little value then forcibly convinced by those governed by fears that silence is not golden but a festering deviance; confusedly growing up into degrading categorizations.

I have seen barely toddling babies' heads experimentally opened up and sliced and drilled then fitted with electrodes, magnets, wires and machines for a life of electrical-cords-coming-out-of-my-head existence to pacify ashamed, scared, unrelenting parents.

I have seen righteous teachers employ a vise of control over crying, frightened, and begging-for-mercy kindergartners making them Show-and-Tell, Show-and-Tell their hearing apparatuses to each and every curious pair of eyes in the classroom; teaching the longstanding mandated "different is wrong."

I have seen dull-eyed parents blankly with hands folded turn to the college-degreed experts, placing their child unresistingly into the ready-to-rescue hands of those tunnelvisioning towards "normalcy."

I have seen the baccalaureated, mastered, and doctor-of-philosophied deaf deeply teeth their lips, fixate a stare on table cracks, press the blood out of their hands while watching protocol take control, another child corralled into the Can't-Be-Me mentality.

I have seen high schoolers sent to face crowds battling peer-pressured acceptance while self-consciously toting obnoxiously bulky headpieces with antennae, boxes with wires, buttons and lights beepingly announcing loudly all the fix-it hopes and standardizationing decrees.

I have seen teenagers fightingly overcompensate, grossly loading on more and more tasks while their parents heartily cheer on the futile battle, both believing somehow, in some way, perhaps there may be a transformation into someone who can fool them all.

I have seen again and again celebration granted to the pretend-
ers shedding the soaringly blessed difference that empowers,
but chooses to hobble weighted down by guilt on the ground
blending into millions.

I have seen limelight-loving, praise-seeking, far-from-qualified,
barely signing interpreters become daytime mothers, a gossip-
ing friend, walking cheat-sheets, a classroom buddy sticking
up in a fight, the mouth, the brain and the life of a solitary but
least restrictively appropriately mainstreamed, inclusioned,
and "so-called-very-close-to-normal" child.

I have seen paternalists reach out hands and hearts to those in
dire need, spartanly donating precious time, energy, and focus,
pastorly citing the benefits of giving without getting, then
turn away with fear, complete puzzlement, confused anger
and incredulous awe from one of us standing, clear-eyed, well
versed, and without need.

I have seen a those-who-can-hear continuum from high school
dropouts to university professors firmly believe Aristotelian
claims that all of us are in all cases incapable of thought or
reason, then wondered as

I have seen rights-fighting groups from all walks terrorize with
fear, making people stammer, intimidated, hurriedly search-
ing for a stable, inoffensive, unmistakable string of words, and
I have enviously desired some of that power while

I saw the cowering, chattering crowd transform Hydelike into
holier-than-thous, turning to spit biting, disapproving
glances at our dramatic expressiveness; the beauty they per-
ceive as freaky animation, our massive expanse of poetic body
cinematics.

I have seen hordes of religious-guided do-gooders from all denom-
inations chase down the poor little deaf souls needing to be
put on a platter and brought to Jesus, and when an elusive one
is caught,

I have seen their looks of smug satisfaction and self-laudation for
so brilliantly conquering one of the lost, dark, unexposed, and
oh so isolated.

I have seen fresh-faced boys and pig-tailed girls wide-eyedly broadcasted, televised before congregations of hundreds and slapped to be cured by babbling pretentious fraudulent fanatics for desperate parents' attempts at the perfect.

I have seen officers of the law handcuff innocents, raping their communication and jeeringly throw them into penned units without the Miranda and held without word or a phone call for hours, or days, and

I have seen ambulances speed to hospitals with good intentions and the nervous doctors' dismissal without tested explanations, then those ER visits followed by hearses with the dishonored luckless riding forever solemn, and

I have seen universities deny intelligent, frequently well-proven abilities a continuing education, some going as far as to alter success to falsify a failure, and

I have seen employers abruptly fire good, diligent, devoted workers in need of little upgrading and

I have seen young children forced by judges to hear and speak for their parents for bankruptcies, for divorces, for criminalities for this and for that and for God knows what else in front of menageried courtrooms, and

I have seen bankers talk loans, doctors talk cancer, dentists talk pain, cashiers talk change, teachers talk progress, and day after day of others use the same child to talk, and

I have seen all of these smilingly excused by "Oh, sorry. An interpreter wasn't in the budget."

I have seen erroneous medicines prescribed on fantastical assumptions passing as diagnoses and further sickness result, many close to death calls.

I have seen those wrongly accused and misexamined, those without the self-protection of language thrown into mental institutions and filed away for decades.

I have seen the young and ambitious fill out scores of applications seeking employment, entrusting faith in new empowering laws, only to be again coldly and regardlessly told, "We don't take your kind."

I have seen nonlethal genocide, the cognitively murdered, a withering, despairing generation of do we have any choices surrenderingly fading lost into the foggy smoke of alcoholcocaineheroinmarijuanamethamphetamines.

I have seen mothers ununderstandingly tricked by the well-intended (such as their own parents) into signing papers legal and binding, unknowingly releasing custody of their children, then sent home in wonderment only to realize days later, heartwreckingly, that they have been rendered childless, vehemently unwilling and with despair must face life without their babies.

I have seen self-servers ride the coattails of their prized model darling's oh-so-delightfully-normal successes, spouting hard-luck stories, profiting fame and fortune off the bridges burned, door shut and confusion beaten amok for many others searching for directions.

I have seen looks of pity and uncomfortable grins, openmouthed stares, twisted expressions, and shunning eyes, all towards an unpleasant disquiet and chuckling anxiety; a discomfort not at all my own.

I have seen tearstained years of speech-training succeed (hallelujah!), to follow with teeth grinding years of learning one must perpetually, constantly, silently, quietly be unmilitantly docile.

I have seen strong-willed individuals crumble in desperation, flailing in frustration, crying out in a fight against helplessness, and straining against steely chains, clinging to stubbornly optimistic desires against constant oppression and ignorance, and

I have seen denials repeatedly Uncle Tom-ed, the wishfully daring becoming fodder for pinching, parroting crabs retrogressingly destroying courage with silence, but

I have seen a degree of intensity unparalleled and lovely, and explosion of unity and tenacious respect; quick perseverance and worldwide pride; an ironclad embrace on a way of life; a passionate loyalty, unmatched, unequalled, unwavering, and loved.

When They Tell Me . . .

When they tell me
    That my thoughts cannot possibly be powerful
    Because my voice cannot create beauty
I feel angry.
But I am not allowed anger
For to be angry is to be defiant.

When they tell me
    That to be good I must be obedient, taciturn, never cause trouble
    To comply gratefully in the face of insults and humiliation
I feel rage.
But I am not allowed rage
For to feel rage is to be a radical.

When they tell me
    I should ashamedly shun the fluency that flows from my hands
    And erase the grotesque emotions and information from my face
I feel revulsion.
But I am not allowed revulsion
For to feel revulsion is to be a disgrace.

When they tell me
    I should pretend to happily conform
    And find satisfaction from a part-time life on the fringe
I feel despair.
But I am not allowed despair
For to feel despair is to be unappreciative.

When they tell me
    That my life of silence has no value, no significance, and no sense
    For easing the way for those too young to know
I feel hate.
But I am not allowed hate
For to feel hate is to be a militant.

When they tell me
    I don't realize how deprived I am, how isolated and behind
    And that my people cannot ever succeed without someone
        holding their hand
I feel aghast.
But I am not allowed aghast
For to feel aghast is to refuse to assimilate.

When they tell me
    I cannot be tenacious, I must accept coercion;
    I cannot be opinionated, I must accept debasement;
    I cannot be intense, I must accept degradation;
    I cannot be confident, I must accept abuse;
    I cannot aspire, I must accept inferiority;
    I am not allowed resentment, I'd be a troublemaker;
    I am not allowed fury, I'd be a rebel;
    I am not allowed horror, I'd be abnormal;
    I am not allowed frustration, I'd be insane;
And if I dare . . .
I'd be diseased.

How dare I?
Oh, do I dare!
I do dare!
    And I can!
But I am not allowed strength
For I am not allowed to be human.

John Lee Clark
(1978–)

PERHAPS BECAUSE HE LED a charmed Deaf childhood with Deaf parents and siblings and was never the only Deaf student at school, John Lee Clark's poetry about his experiences with signing and Deaf culture is free of angst. "Story Actual Happen," based on a story about one of his intimate role models, the superb storyteller and American Sign Language (ASL) lyricist Taras J. Dykstra, is an example of the faithful ASL gloss style Clark uses in some of his work. Stories such as the one told in "Long Goodbyes" epitomize a hallmark of Deaf culture—the leave-taking rituals that stretch on for hours. However, this is changing as Deaf people have more access to long-distance communication, making their meetings in person less sacred, which is why this is a nostalgic poem.

In "The Only Way Signing Can Kill Us," Clark satirizes mainstream society's romantic ideas that signing is like drawing pictures in the air. As slyly humorous as this poem is, it does suggest that such notions are harmful. He continues his intellectual playfulness in "My Understanding One Day of Foxgloves" by acknowledging that nature does make mistakes and explaining that if deafness is one of them, it is quite natural.

John Lee Clark was born deaf in St. Paul, Minnesota, to a Deaf mother and a DeafBlind father. By sixth grade, when he transferred from a Deaf program at a public school to the Minnesota State Academy for the Deaf (MSAD), he was legally blind. After graduating from MSAD in 1997, he studied briefly at Gallaudet University before he and his wife started a family and established a publishing venture. For six years, they ran The Tactile Mind Press, which produced books and DVDs of signing community literature.

Clark's writings appear in many publications, among them *Ache*, *The Deaf-Blind American*, *McSweeney's*, and *Sign Language Studies*, and he is the first signer, Deaf or DeafBlind, to be published in the prestigious magazine *Poetry*. The only DeafBlind artist featured at the Deaf Way II International Cultural Arts Festival, he is the recipient of the Robert F. Panara Award for Poetry and many grants. In 2005, he edited the anthology *Clayton: A Tribute to Clayton Valli*, and his first collection of poems, *Suddenly Slow*, appeared in 2008. Currently, he is the director of Communication Facilitator Services with Hawk Relay.

Story Actual Happen

after Taras J. Dykstra

Me remember longago 1967
Gallaudet. Acrossstreet
Italian Restaurant mouthwatering.
Buddies us "¿Want? Sure!"

Seataround: relax cuttingup.
Me story *jokes*. Laughter.
Waitress arrive. Me gape:
beautiful luscious shapely
black woman. "¿Drink?"

Wow. Too sexy, me can't seduce.
Turnturn order drinks.
Then myturn: me squeeze
(on breast) like sign "milk."
Black woman expression,
vanish. Buddies they pointme:
"Dare! Awful you!"
Snicker, elbow nudge.

Me more story *jokes*.
Waitress *back*, servedrinks
turnturn, except me nothing.
I wave her "¿Huh?"
She smile, gesture wait.

Finally she *back*, handover
tallglass. Me gape.
Neckswallow me, whew.
Not milk. ¿Know what?

Chocolate milk.

Long Goodbyes

I miss all of the long goodbyes
of my parents' guests
taking their leave by not leaving

when it was time to go. Someone would sign
Better go home we but hours would pass
around our round table—

the bowls of our hands offering
confession after confession
assuring us that we are we—

before anyone stands up.
Then others, sighing, will stand up
slowly and slowly walk

through our house, pausing
where the walls offer stories,
reasons to stay longer

and touch more things with our hands.
I remember how long,
how wonderfully they stood

unwilling to open the front door,
signing away with warm faces
and hugging goodbye again

before going gently into the night.
My family would huddle to watch
their cars' headlights roll away

but pause to flash in the Deaf way,
waving goodbye to our house.
How we children dashed inside

to light switches for our house
to wave back goodbye,
light to light bright in the night!

Now that I am grown
and have my own family, do come
for a visit but do not leave
when it is time to go. Sign, do sign
Better go home we and our hands
will make time go suddenly slow.

The Only Way Signing Can Kill Us

would be if the world took
a fancy to the way
certain signs made images
and the world would try
to have things be more
like pictures in the air.

To begin with, there would
be only one season, winter,
because the signs
for the other seasons
do not give the idea
the way winter does,
our arms bent and shivering.

And that endless winter would
freeze us to death,
mainly because our house
would have only two walls.

It might as well be,
since all trees would
have five leafless branches
that never bear fruit,
which we would not need
anyway, since food would
only kiss our lips coyly,
knowing that swallowing
occurs on, not in, our throats.

Naturally, we would try
to live in spite of all this
by making fire, for us to drink
life, life from its light,
but it would be hopeless:
our flames would not
be fierce enough and would,
as our arms stiffen,
be too much like the sign
for waiting, which we would
be, waiting for death.

Still, still, we are happy:
There is only one way
signing can kill us,
and everything else it can
ever hope to make is life.

My Understanding One Day of Foxgloves

for Douglass Bullard

I was gardening hand and foot,
my mind handinglove
with foxgloves,
when out of the blue
a rush of wind mistook me
for something much lighter.

Bowled over foot over hand
and about to fly,
I felt for my foxgloves
and they took hold of my fingers
by the thimble, fingertip
in fingerhut—small wonder
their kind is called *Digitalis*
and their kindness dumb love.

They paid no mind to nature
calling them
to unhand yours truly,
here mute but gloved.

I smiled at the sky
between my feet, knowing
that my foxgloves are true,
truer to my fingers
than any mistake of nature.

My understanding has some weight,
so my feet will soon glissade
down to earth, to rest again
close to my hands
cuddling small wonders.

Kristen Ringman
(1979–)

Reading Kristen Ringman's "the ear gods," one may be puzzled at how she would know what the "faceless ears in the sky" are telling her if she cannot hear them. The answer is simple: there are levels ranging from merely hearing to listening. Deaf people have always been aware of what society tells them, but that doesn't always mean they buy it. While it may be a disadvantage that Deaf people have limited access to mainstream society, one advantage is that mainstream society, in turn, has only limited access to Deaf people. This is why Ringman is able to tell hearing people to go ahead and walk over her, since she would "rather be against the Earth," away from them.

In "Calling Van Gogh," Ringman continues to distinguish between multiple levels of "hearing." As dim a view as she holds for ears, she is not afraid to accuse a Deaf man who raped her of not hearing her signing "No," just like many men who do not hear women voice their "no." This step away from the Deaf Pride movement's virtuous front, its insistence that Deaf people can do no wrong, is a relatively recent development in the community's literature. "Deaf people can be scum, too," as Christopher Jon Heuer declares.

Kristen Ringman was born with full hearing in Providence, Rhode Island, to a deaf mother who speaks and reads lips. Beginning at the age of six, Ringman gradually became deaf and was profoundly deaf by the time she reached college. She graduated from the University of New Hampshire in 2001 with a bachelor's degree in English and studio art. Although she began learning American Sign Language at thirteen, she did not use it until her early twenties.

Since college, she has done mural painting in India, Kenya, and Ireland, as well as in the United States. Ringman is also a freelance photographer and a certified herbalist. Between 1999 and 2005, she spent a total of one year in India, mostly working with the late Ann Plummer of Auroville, an international community in Tamil Nadu, where they cared for stray dogs. In 2005, she illustrated the memoir of Lama Chimpa, a Mongolian nomad monk. In 2008, she graduated from the Goddard College Master of Fine Arts Program in Creative Writing and completed her first novel.

the ear gods

standing up on that stage
where I could speak without needing
to hear
it was the only place where the ear gods
couldn't find me
I grew up praying to them
the faceless ears in the sky
they told me I had to be faceless too
"don't show that feeling"
"don't touch that person with your heart"
they said
but thank Goddess, I couldn't hear
I couldn't hear all that bullshit
their faces didn't have mouths
their lips couldn't tell me stories
about how wonderful the sounds
of intelligible words could be
people look away
and have hour-long conversations
without even glancing
into eyes that hold too much
of something
into hands that could tell better stories
like hearts overflowing
sorry if I've bumped into you
my heart tends
to knock people over
I stumble but at least I can see
where I'm falling
I can feel the sound of my head
against the ground
and you can walk over me
I'd rather be against the Earth

I'd rather be inside the dirt
enveloped
where the ear gods
will never find me
again.

Calling Van Gogh*

I called Van Gogh this morning
Forgetting that I was Deaf
And he
Didn't have ears
And thought
What an idea!
My ears didn't work anyway
Could I donate them to a hospital?
Could I feed them to a bear in the woods?
I think I'd rather they were eaten
Like the sounds people chew and spit out
Before I can possibly grasp a hint
Of their flavor
I'd ask a man how the sound of the word
NO
Can taste
Because the time I needed that most
I was with a Deaf man
Who wouldn't watch my hands that said
NO
So I doubt he ever learned
How it tasted
I doubt most men listen
When they hear that sound
Much less swallow it
I think they'd rather choke
And spit it out like
A bear might spit out the bones
Of my ears
And the next time I need a man to
Taste

* Vincent Van Gogh (1853–1890) was a Dutch post-Impressionist painter who sliced off his ear in a fit of rage.

The word NO
I can carve it into a piece of bone
And shove it down his throat
That'll help him taste it
That'll help me run away
From men that don't listen
And ears that don't hear.

Alison L. Aubrecht
(1979–)

As THE EXODUS OF deaf children from residential schools continues, and most hearing parents continue to neither learn American Sign Language nor include their deaf children fully in the family, the signing community is being flooded with young adults, some very angry, who are seeking to clarify their identities and to protest against the injustices they bore growing up. Unlike mainstreamed students of earlier generations, these young people have access to stronger cultural and political literature, which the Deaf Pride movement has produced. Further, at Gallaudet and many other colleges, Deaf studies courses have given names and explanations to what students have suffered, such as communication abuse, educational neglect, and audism.

Much of Alison L. Aubrecht's clear and straightforward poetry is an indictment against family and teachers, testifying to the psychological and sometimes physical repercussions of audism. A strong sense of loss and longing runs through her work—rage at the loss of missed chances and longing for communication with family, for meaningful learning, and, in "Hearing-Headed" (a reference to an ASL slang sign meaning someone who is deaf but acts hearing), for the dream of one day signing freely, being openly and happily Deaf.

Alison Leigh Aubrecht was born in Saint Louis Park, Minnesota. Her elementary and secondary education was spent in mainstream programs at public schools. Aubrecht entered Gallaudet University in 1997 and earned a bachelor's degree in psychology and a master's degree in mental health. She has worked at the Michigan School for the Deaf and the Model Secondary School for the Deaf as a counselor. Aubrecht directed the popular *Audism Monologues*, a play aimed at raising awareness about audism. Her writings, both poetry and essays on social issues, appear widely.

ape-child

she sits at her desk
in a secluded classroom
which consists of only
six students

the teacher speaks
loud and clear
and they squint their eyes
desperately trying to keep up
failing to read every word

in the back of her mind
a tiny voice screams
for escape from this
prison of the soul

during break
she finds herself gesturing
with another classmate
only to have a ruler

SLAM down on her hands

SHUTTING OUT HER SPIRIT

tears well up in her eyes
as she wonders why it's so wrong
when it feels so right
but pride prevents them from falling
this time

would you do this to your child
would you take her heart and squash it
would you leave it up to teachers to beat her hands
would you tell her its wrong to try anything short of speaking
to learn a language
would you spend hours teaching her how to say a word correctly
instead of holding her in your arms tenderly
would you tell her to make you proud
by making her do something so painful

at night she goes home
and closes her eyes,
her head aching from the effort
and her heart yearning
nearly bursting
from the lacking

in the dim light
her mother tucks her in
and says, "good night honey.
I love you."

But she does not see.

Conditional Wings

i have longed
To be a part of you, family
So deeply that it hurt like hell
And to protect myself, my body
Formed anger, resentment, pride
And i regressed into a child
Demanding attention

i was always in the way
Too difficult
Or too special
Too spoiled
Or too temperamental
Unappreciative

Of all the tokens given to me
The books i'd never read
Because you didn't bother to discover
The titles that were my passion
The clothes i'd never wear
Because they didn't suit the soul
You couldn't ever know
For lack of meaningful conversations

The money spent
Recklessly in attempt to fill
The emptiness inside of me
Here, don't talk, here's a dollar
i've never wanted for things
But how i've longed
To feel the love i saw

In the conversations you shared, family
In your laughter and tears
You gave me wings but no directions
Because—of course,
How could i possibly fly?

What My Teacher Taught Me

when i was just starting out
a child surrounded by
those who bow to sound
you put me in front of the class
and mandated that I speak
your excitement plausible
and the faces in front of me
smirking or puzzled or pitying
you gave me a super sticker
a pat on the head and beamed at me
all afternoon

you taught me that
i was as good as my willingness
to use my voice
even when others didn't understand me
even when i couldn't express myself
you taught me that communication
is one sided

when i was plodding through
struggling with puberty
you forced me to sit in the front
and spoke to my interpreter, facing her
you said, "Tell her she can stop anytime
if this assignment becomes too hard"
you watched the signs pass through the air
and when motion became stillness
glanced at my forehead then walked away

you taught me that
leaving someone alone in humiliation
is acceptable
you taught me that i was
somebody you couldn't connect with
a thrift-store underwear kid
and you taught me that
it's okay to give up

when i was a young adult
starting to understand the intricacies
of perspectives, attitudes, and behaviors
you told me i couldn't succeed without your help
that if i didn't let you revise my paper
i'd fail and when i aced anyway
you told me i cheated
and then you spoke in front of me
but when i asked you what you said
i was brushed off, "Oh, it's not important"

you taught me that i could never
live up to the potential that i felt
burning inside of me
that someone else controls
whether or not I have a chance
you taught me that i didn't
have the right to decide for myself
what was interesting or important

when i was almost done
creeping close to the day i'd
endeavor out into "the real world"
i reported the abuse i saw
and you told them i was mentally ill
that i was out of control and crazy
(forgetting that i could filter
the poison that falls from your lips)

you taught me to cover up
to lie and cheat to stay in the game
you taught me that it was wrong
to fight for those weaker than me
and right to squash them along the way

those are just some of the smaller lessons,
dear teacher
just some of the lighter bruises
the slighter scars
that i write of today

you put them there
hidden deep where no one could see
believe

you taught me, teacher
to bruise back.

The Ghost in Yellowed Photographs

To my father

All those times you shunned me
Because I was too hard to communicate with
All those times you preferred him to me
Because he could hear you better
All those never minds you threw at me
Resulted in me not knowing who you really are

Now that you're dead
Tears for a sweet stranger
Forever fall.

Hearing-Headed

Softly slicing the cold air
Your hands fly
A stark contrast to the stillness
Of this sheltered room.

Shamelessly, your face
Wrenches with emotion
Bared free for the
Whole world to see.

Without motion i watch you
Half humiliated
Somewhat astounded
And long to be you.

i struggle with wanting
To move fluidly
Open up visually so that i may
Communicate clearly

And feeling rooted
In an expressionless
Frozen state
Of flat noise.

Turning a cheek
Choking back a tear
i sit on my hands
For now, i will only dream.

Bibliography

Burnet, John R. *Tales of the Deaf and Dumb, with Miscellaneous Poems*. Newark, NJ: Benjamin Olds, 1835.

Clark, John Lee. *Suddenly Slow: Poems*. Minneapolis: Handtype Press, 2008.

———, ed. *Clayton: A Tribute to Clayton Valli*. Minneapolis: The Tactile Mind Press, 2005.

Cook, Peter. "Don Quoxitie Didnt Really Attack the Windmill," in *Action No. 7*, May 1986.

Fuller, Angeline A. *The Venture*. Detroit: J. N. Williams, 1883.

Garretson, Mervin D. *Words from a Deaf Child*. Silver Spring, MD: Fragonard Press, 1984.

Golladay, Loy E. *A Is for Alice*. Hartford, CT: American School for the Deaf, 1991.

Hanson, Agatha Tiegel. Privately published collection.

Heuer, Christopher Jon. *All Your Parts Intact: Poems*. Minneapolis: The Tactile Mind Press, 2003.

Hodgson, Edwin Allan, ed. *Facts, Anecdotes, and Poetry Relating to the Deaf and Dumb*. New York: Deaf-Mutes' Journal, 1891.

Jennings, Alice Cornelia. *My Queen*. (Two copies available in the Gallaudet University Library.)

Jepson, Jill, ed. *No Walls of Stone: An Anthology of Literature by Deaf and Hard-of-Hearing Writers*. Washington, DC: Gallaudet University Press, 1992.

Kowalewski, Felix. *You and I*. Riverside, CA: California School for the Deaf, 1983.

Krentz, Christopher, ed. *A Mighty Change: An Anthology of Deaf American Writing, 1816–1864*. Washington, DC: Gallaudet University Press, 2000.

Jones, Judy Yaeger, and Jane E. Vallier, eds. *Sweet Bells Jangled: Laura Redden Searing: A Deaf Poet Restored*. Washington, DC: Gallaudet University Press, 2003.

Long, J. Schuyler. *Out of the Silence: A Book of Verse*. Council Bluffs, IA: Author, 1908.

Lowman, Rex. *Bitterweed*. Belle Vista, AR: Belle Vista Press, 1964.

Luczak, Raymond. *St. Michael's Fall: Poems*. Rochester, NY: Deaf Life Press, 1996.

McFarlane, J. H., and Howard L. Terry, comps. *Poems by the Deaf : An Anthology*. In collaboration with Kate S. Shibley, 1942. (One copy available in the Gallaudet University Archives.)

McVan, Alice Jane. *Tryst*. New York: Hispanic Society of America, 1953.

Miles, Dorothy. *Gestures: Poetry in American Sign Language*. Northridge, CA: Joyce Motion Picture Co., 1976.

Nack, James. *The Legend of the Rocks, and Other Poems*. New York: E. Conrad, 1827.

Panara, Robert F. *On His Deafness and Other Melodies Unheard*. Rochester, NY: Deaf Life Press, 1997.

Smith, Linwood. *Silence, Love, and Kids I Know: Poems*. Silver Spring, MD: National Association of the Deaf, 1979.

Sollenberger, Earl. *Along With Me*. Paterson, NJ: Gayren Press, 1937.

———. *Handful of Quietness*. Paterson, NJ: Gayren Press, 1941.

Sowell, James William. *To Her I Love*. Omaha: Privately published, 1948.

Teegarden, George Moredock. *Vagrant Verses*. Fanwood, NY: Fanwood Press, 1929.

Terry, Howard L. *Sung in Silence*. Los Angeles: Author, 1929.

Wright-Meinhardt, Pamela. "A Letter to C. F." In *The Deaf Way II Anthology: A Literary Collection by Deaf and Hard of Hearing Writers*, edited by Tonya M. Stremlau, 139–141. Washington, DC: Gallaudet University Press, 2002.